OTHER GIRLS TO BURN

Association of
Writers & Writing Programs
Award for Creative
Nonfiction

OTHER
GIRLS TO
BURN

Caroline Crew

The University of Georgia Press

ATHENS

Published by the University of Georgia Press
Athens, Georgia 30602
www.ugapress.org
© 2021 by Caroline Crew
All rights reserved
Designed by Erin Kirk
Set in Arno
Printed and bound by Sheridan Books
The paper in this book meets the guidelines for
permanence and durability of the Committee on
Production Guidelines for Book Longevity of the
Council on Library Resources.

Most University of Georgia Press titles are
available from popular e-book vendors.

Printed in the United States of America

21 22 23 24 25 P 5 4 3 2 1

Library of Congress Cataloging-in-Publication Data
Names: Crew, Caroline, author.
Title: Other girls to burn / Caroline Crew.
Description: Athens, Georgia : The University of Georgia Press,
[2021] | Includes bibliographical references.
Identifiers: LCCN 2021018803 (print) | LCCN 2021018804 (ebook) |
ISBN 9780820360430 (paperback) | ISBN 9780820360447 (ebook)
Subjects: LCSH: Crew, Caroline. | Women—Identity. | Sex role. |
Violence—Psychological aspects.
Classification: LCC HQ1233 .C746 2020 (PRINT) | LCC HQ1233
(EBOOK) | DDC 155.6/423—dc23
LC record available at https://lccn.loc.gov/2021018803
LC ebook record available at https://lccn.loc.gov/2021018804

For Zoe Rana Mungin

We stand on the rim of the void.

I massed all of my grief at my mutilator's feet.
No, sweetheart,
   he said,

that's yours.

We hold our little lamps of knowing
on the rim, and look in.

—Molly Brodak, "Materialism," *The Cipher* (2020)

CONTENTS

OTHER GIRLS TO BURN

RELIQUARY

First Class

I only Google "foreskins" for Jesus.

Though we know he was circumcised, the scope of Christ's foreskin is debatable. According to some accounts, there were as many as eighteen relics of the Holy Prepuce claimed throughout medieval Europe. A relic of this order—directly related to Christ, or the physical remains of a saint—is First Class. Of all the foreskins with which I have been familiar, none have attained the status of First Class. Of all the foreskins with which I have been familiar, I hope it's true I have not considered any of them objects.

To be a relic, a body must be done. Done living, done changing, done with its sovereignty. When becoming an object, a body must submit to stasis.

The bodies of saints not anatomized for individual relics—and one must consider the economic benefits of some holy butchery—have become objects by stopping. Their holiness preserved in the act of preservation. The "incorrupt" corpses of saints have, in part, gained sainthood by dint of the miracle of refusing to rot. What supernatural or sly human intervention has kept these corpses incorrupt is largely unknown. A miracle against the ordinariness of death. Stopped time.

To be incorrupt is first a matter of bodies—it is only a few centuries later that the term comes to describe character. The body comes before the moral. But an object, an object can't offer a moral we don't assign.

Second Class

There is a healthy traffic of holy relics on eBay. These are more likely to be Second Class (an object owned or worn by a saint) or Third Class (an object touched by Christ or a saint). Authenticity aside, the Holy Prepuce is unlikely to be found at auction. Or, at all. In 1900, the Catholic Church ruled anyone found discussing any one of Christ's foreskins would be excommunicated. The last surviving Holy Prepuce, located in Calcata, Italy, was stolen in 1983. It seems the thief was never found—or perhaps feared being ejected from the Church's embrace by confessing.

When a body becomes an object, its meaning is only ascribed by other bodies. A body in motion might mean many things, an object stopped in time has only a singular significance. A static history.

I don't believe in Christ, but I do believe in history.

I don't believe in the object, but I do believe in the body.

Third Class

If you must imagine the Holy Foreskin still survives, look upward. Prefiguring the Church's lockdown on this most intimate of relics, seventeenth-century theologian Leo Allatius declared all Holy Prepuces fakes—the true foreskin of Christ had quit this mortal coil and transcended to space. The rings of Saturn, that was the true location of what remains of Christ's cock. A body so stopped in time it's frozen in light-years. Starlit forever.

A relic of the past. When referring to a person, perhaps whose views are archaic or abhorrent, as a "relic," we attempt to place that person in a history that refuses any connection to the present. We want to stop time, isolate its horrors.

But history is a body, not an object. It moves, and rots and corrupts, and moves on.

Recent relics, according to the headlines: manufacturing, soap operas, marital rape, herbal medicine, mail delivery, national identity, moral relativism, a home-cooked meal, slavery, ethernet cables, ambassadors, religion. It is easier to believe in relics than it is to believe in a body. Bodies change. Bodies corrupt.

Let me rot, so I may change.

A perfect relic might outlast us all. Perhaps, somewhere lost, someone will still be awed by the shriveled sliver of Jesus's foreskin when my corpse is decaying without the odor of sanctity. That scrap might be stashed in the most perfect jeweled box, inlaid with mother of pearl—emeralds and rubies and a flash of opal. Safe and static, without the weight of time, of history.

The Church no longer accepts incorruptibility as a miracle.

I AM A BURNING GIRL

Wrapped in the good bleach, the house becomes both border and brine. On a dance floor, a little dirt is good for bodies to grip. You hold on. I hold on to anger.

As a stoke for flame, feeling is sufficient.

We are taught that good fuel must be renewable. Case study: Throughout the nineteenth century the underglow of beauty ate so many girls it became known as "the holocaust of ballet girls." Not *ballerinas* (previously this has been used sparingly as a term to denote supreme accomplishment), but *girls*. The gas lamps on stage illuminated the work of their limbs: limbs fine-molded; lovely limbs; limbs framed ugly with flame protection.

A good ballet girl has not soaked her muslin dress in alum, lets layers fly. Grace is more alluring in ghosts than in girls. Both is big bucks.

Previously known as melancholy, this phenomenon is now called media. Remake them more beautiful, moths to a flame. Destined. A tragic destiny. We neglect to look at our own hands, newsprint-stained and fingers on the TV remote, writing the narrative for these girls. I take a burning selfie of oven-gained scars. I make my hair a burning color: case study in victim performance.

I think, *I am a burning girl.*

Though the power will not go out in this week of June storms, I build pyres for safety. I could make church candles from the unacceptable fat in my ass. Fuel is a finite resource only in constructed borders.

The moon will not light. We have other girls to burn for us.

Within the smoke it is difficult to distinguish specific figures. They could be Saints Thea and Valentina—in AD 308 brought before the governor of Palestine. He, weary of torture, commands that the torn up virgins be bound together and burned on the same fire. Fuel-efficient. Many others burn.

They could be Saints Agape, Chionia, and Irene, meaning "love," "purity," and "peace" in Greek. These sisters refused sacred food, were bodies refusing their machine part, and so got burned.

We have other girls to burn for us.

Saints Justa and Rufina, more sisters, more fuel (though after expiring from other methods).

Joan of Arc, everyone's sister, burned.

A fuel might burn outside its expected spectrum of yellow, orange, red, depending on impurities surrounding and inherent, but annihilation is certain. Copper burns blue and green. Sugar burns blue.

An exemplar of asset, Saint Afra, her body defined as capital and not a natural resource—a product of her mother's work, was an early model for the importance of adaptability in enterprise. Sold into sacred prostitution in the Temple of Venus, the body of Afra later converts to Christian fuel. Though she sacrifices herself to Christ, she is not her own to give.

We light candles to ask them for help, these women we kill.

I was not raised Catholic but light a candle for the dead in every church I can. It is the limit of my own spectrum that I remember these only as red or white. In Amsterdam I visit Oude Kerk cathedral, consecrated in 1306 and situated in the city's current red-light district. Here I light a white candle so that my father will not die before I get home for Christmas. At the time, the cathedral is also home to *The Museum of Broken Relationships*, debris given proper pause. I wonder if I have burned the right shade.

Later, when I get accustomed to lighting candles to signify *love, I am sorry*, the apologies hinge on the confession that I could burn, too.

Despite having lived in Massachusetts for two years, this is my first visit to Salem. We visit the museum, which is, really, not a museum in the sense of housing artifacts but a museum in that it defines itself as "the Salem Witch Museum." It offers terrible dioramas with a B-movie voiceover. Though we could expect more from the primary museum in Salem, we want the circus as well as the history.

The sideshow freaks center staged: femme fatales now flaming. The truth is that no one burned at Salem. The truth is that we want to remember witches burning.

A full culture's dream: To watch a hanging in your dream represents feelings of insecurity. The hanging may symbolize aspects of yourself that you want to eliminate. To dream that someone is being burned alive suggests that you are being consumed by your own ambition.

We must be a nation of consumers.

But I wasn't there to discuss how the emergence of pre–Industrial Age capitalism might have been the trigger for the English witch hunts or how difficult it is to view this as a movie with end credits considering the news going on outside.

This news is the Isla Vista shooting, in which Elliot Rodger murdered six people as a result of deep misogyny, but it could and will be substituted for numerous other nameable and unnamed events.

The unnamable of Salem are numerous.

In the museum not a single woman who was hanged was named (some of those who lounged in prison or were released still not knowing their crimes got a catcall, others were referred to as "wife of . . ."). However, every man who died, whether through torture or hanging, was named. An entire diorama was devoted to Giles Corey, *his* strength, *his* bravery, *his* pain. Martha, *his* wife, hanged and killed, again as a footnote.

John Proctor's pregnant wife, who was subject to the same punishment as him but granted a stay of execution because of her condition, was only named as wife. He was named as "one of the few brave *men*" who stood against the hysteria.

Hysteria has not been erased. *Hysteria* meaning, fundamentally, "of the womb." The displacement or misuse of this female anatomical element, like any transgression of female bodies, is an aberration. This disease originally thought to be caused from unwanted sexual abstinence found its cure in sex. The clinical becomes the clerical and so the womb becomes the demon. What Tertullian calls "the devil's gateway" lets in mortal and moral sickness.

Returning home after Salem I am grateful. I call out my female friends as coven, I name them. We name each other against our erasures. We name those women murdered at Salem: Bridget Bishop, Rebecca Nurse, Sarah Good, Susannah Martin, Elizabeth Howe, Sarah Wildes, Martha Carrier, Martha Corey, Mary Eastey, Ann Pudeator, Alice Parker, Mary Parker, Margaret Scott, Sarah Osborn, Lyndia Dustin, Ann Foster. We name those being murdered still: George Chen, Cheng Yuan "James" Hong, Weihan "David" Wang, Katherine Breann Cooper, Christopher Ross Michaels-Martinez, Veronika Elizabeth Weiss.

We gasp for air, we stoke the fire with our breath.

THE DISCOMFORT INDEX

↓

There is no personal space in Vegas. It's like they got to the desert boundary of their Mojave oasis and realized they had to turn back, fold in on themselves, maximize the limited resources, and cram. In the tidal weeknight crowd by the Bellagio fountain, the canopy cover gives one man the opportunity to grope me at the crosswalk and fade into the crowd before I can turn to see whose hands grabbed my ass. I drove over a thousand miles to get here, and suddenly America is small. Hemmed in.

✳

Our second night in Vegas, the clock ticks to spectacle again. We head out to Olympic Garden, a strip club that promises a male revue, a new experience for us as a couple, and one of the more fun attempts at navigating gender parity in our relationship. Traffic on Sahara Avenue keeps us with our enthusiastic cab driver for an hour, draining the buzz we've built. My boyfriend takes over the cab's stereo to put on the only song he can play on the piano, Against Me!'s "Baby I'm an Anarchist." Holding on to the last of our drunken glow, yelling in tandem, "No, I won't take your hand and marry the State," I allowed myself the naive idea that we were radically rewriting our heteronormative script of love. We're too late. We arrive at Olympic Garden just before 1:00 a.m., sober. The male revue has closed, so instead we settle by the stage, wishing for something other than eleven-dollar Budweisers, and slip back into the regular script.

✳

The discomfort index refers to the comfort of a place based on its humidity, how much air is in the room. In the Vegas strip club, our air is perfectly regulated, a museum, interrupted only by the display. For these few hours, I am not the only woman as a spectator. A small rotation of us keeps up throughout the night, our number waxing and waning, not only through the curtained front doors, but also by the veils drawn back by the dancers themselves.

In the bathroom, I double-take the brunette who had been on the stage two songs ago. I catch her eye in the mirror as we both soap our hands; her smile, now different, now warm, opens the multitude: How many of these women are there? How many roles must we play? How many of those roles have we written ourselves?

To be a sex object is to be emptied and rebuilt as a prop for someone else's desire. Almost every dancer that takes the stage makes me her understudy. I am pawed and praised, my breasts no longer personal property, my glasses removed so that my face may fold into clavicles and cleavage. If all this world's a stage, I'm a prop for its lead actresses.

✳

If Vegas is the spandex and choreography of professional wrestling, Atlanta's strip clubs are the raw beauty of boxing. The Clermont Lounge is the oldest and most legendary strip club in Atlanta. It was, for a brief time, my most beloved college haunt. Among the many things I learned at that tiny dive bar with two-dollar beer was that a woman could set her nipples on fire, and that I was ready to love my body.

The women of the Clermont were not the stereotyped performers of the public (or private) imagination, but they staked their own stars in the constellation of age, size, color. And though the economy of attention was a swamp for me to wade through, one that I didn't understand at that point, twenty-two and far from home, I could see past the smoke and dollar bills and knew that they, all these women, were adored.

I have a certain nostalgia for the Clermont, that much I've made obvious, but in the glare of excitement, I neglected to see what made this a significant space: not just inclusion, but comfort.

*

The city of Las Vegas was founded on May 15, 1905, the festival of the Roman god Mercury. Mercury: the messenger. Also: patron of financial gain, commerce, travelers, trickery, luck. It is easy for any Las Vegas story to become a fable. In Las Vegas you can go to New York or Paris or Venice: a microcosm of the Western world. It's the capital of capital. When it comes to *what happens in Vegas*, it is wise to remember that other cliché, *don't shoot the messenger.*

*

The messengers here undulate in various forms of undress. A weeknight in Vegas, with no convention in town, means Olympic Garden is almost empty. The dancers move toward us with more than gravity. They reach the boundary of my boyfriend's person and stop. With me, they keep going. They touch me just as they touch themselves.

I do not want this attention. In the same way that chips are not real money, advances here are only a facsimile of affection. And yet, I do not say no. I do not whip my head as I did on the street, eyes fired to find the perpetrator, a lecture loaded on the tongue.

In this economy of attention, perhaps it is foolish to complain of free services rendered. The men of the club tip more, buy more drinks, upgrade to a VIP suite to receive this type of attention. That I receive it for free does not make me a blessed consumer, it tells me I have no power to consume at all.

*

Discomfort comes to modern English from the Old French *descomforter*: "to sadden, to annihilate." Comfort is a tricky concept, a privilege of a concept; one does not notice it until its lack. Less flashy than joy, a duller bird than pain. However, we are taught shame, not discomfort, exactly, in response to nudity, and one does not feel annihilated by shame. Shame glares its light on us, blaringly restates our presence in the situation.

So it is not shame I feel, not expressly, at being touched by Olympic Garden's strippers. Not yet. Discomfort; to be annihilated. In a moment that comes closest to breaking my polite veneer of spectatorship, a woman writhes her body up my torso and licks my mouth. Unprompted, a stranger licks my mouth. Our mouths connect, but our eyes do not. She is looking at him, the man next to me; the person *we* are performing for. No longer a spectator, I am part of the show. The attention I'm given is not for free—it's a ploy for tips elsewhere. Annihilated from person to prop. This is when the shame comes. The red glare apparent on my face despite the dimmed lights.

How can I say to this woman, who understands us both as sex objects in the world we are given, *Not me*? What right do I have to draw the line between us—*I am not a prop for his entertainment, but you are. You may use your body for this, but not mine. I am different.* And would either of us pretend in that utterance that *different* does not make its meaning as *better*?

And who among the two of us is wiser? A woman clinging to arbitrary difference, still groped in the streets, who that morning had worn lingerie her boyfriend bought her, a visual treat; or the woman who sees the fundamental sameness, the single level at which the men of the club regard us?

✳

Devils Point is Portland's self-proclaimed rock 'n' roll strip club. Not mythic, but still supernatural. Less red-velvet occult, more neon and chains and nipple-piercing-grazing crop tops. It seems the devil is in the details: before patrons enter the club beneath the flashing cartoonish Satan, the bouncer politely addresses the boundaries. The rules are sharply drawn: no touching, dollar per song minimum tip, don't ask for special attention if it isn't offered. Punter, bouncer, bartender, stripper—where each of us began and ended, as well as the spaces between us, were clearly and concisely charted.

The club's clouded light could not fog the slick aerial swipes of legs snaking and arching from poles, entrancing me easily. Skin glowed perfectly, unblurred by handprints, as the drone of the music was totally lost in the rhythm of wanting more revealed.

Outside for a cigarette break, one of the dancers and I discussed yoga practice as comfortably as acquaintances wasting time in the elevator.

✳

There is no Olympic Garden of myth. At least, none that my crude study can find. Like Vegas itself, the club is a facsimile of a myth that never quite existed.

∗

When myth returns for me, it's my dad who is the messenger. A moment, perhaps, to explain my father. Strangers have always assumed he's my grandfather. Because he was in his sixties when I was born, this is not a rude assumption. My father is a man of his generation and so not given to turning out his inner life. But dreams—he has a prophet's fascination for dreams.

I don't believe I ever received the birds and the bees talk from my parents, but when I was old enough, my dad told me his worst young nightmare, still clear in his memory from his teenage years during World War II. In the dream, a Women's Land Army member he'd been seeing, Jeanine, stripped for him in the barn and they fell together, entwined. He felt her skin underneath him change, become thick and soft. He looked down to see her transform into a tiger. Then she mauled him. This dream shook him so much he ended their relationship. Those are the mythic creatures I was given to understand sex.

Is this so different to the myths that strip clubs sell us? Or the fairy tale of the porn magazine left in the hedge by the railway station? Eventually, we all rely on archetypes. So, when the myths return for me, it's my dad who is the messenger. I ask him, "Have the doctors confirmed heart surgery?" And he tells me he's been dreaming again, a deflecting though affirmative answer to the question. Of course, he is anxious, but a yes would be too much of a defeat.

Instead, he says he's been dreaming of "*my*-thology." That's how he mispronounces the word, stretching it out like he's still chewing on it. Like a prophet, he says he didn't know the word before it came into his dreams, dreams that spewed forth "awful creatures" writhing into horrible stories and a city he was glad he dreamed was ruined. So, I tell him the awful stories I have learned because I never knew the myths, either. After he hangs up, I wonder—if we aren't given myths when we're young, do we make them for ourselves?

In my crude study, I discover that Mercury, the winged messenger, was also the god of boundaries. A psychopomp guiding souls through the veil from one world to the next. In his guarding of this most opaque boundary, Mercury was charged with taking the loquacious but beautiful nymph Lara to Hades. After she gossips about Jupiter's passions, Jupiter rips out her tongue and sends the silenced Lara out of sight, out of mind. On the way to Hades, Mercury rapes and impregnates the nymph incapable of saying no. In stalking his own boundaries, Mercury ignores those that he should not cross.

I learn to be weary of the stories of women in myths as much as in my daily life. Weary of Leda and Cassandra and Antiope, wearied of the rapes of Philomena and Callisto and Europa. Weary of these messengers. Weary enough to start muttering my own name and those of the women who have storied my life. Weariness can be a comfort, the security blanket numbly fondled, a dull safe place.

The book that teaches me these stories has a kindly lens on the plethora of sexual violence in the pantheon. The author suggests that these stories were an offering of comfort to real women, that it is not their fault; even a goddess is nothing when held in affection by a god. As with much kindness, it is deeply crushing. I hesitate in calling them myths. They might be supernatural, but these rape narratives are, at base, fundamentally ordinary. Everyday.

*

Too often, I have used love to rationalize and subsume discomfort. My father knows very little about my life or work because I love him. And because I love him, I love his comfort, and above all, the comfort of his being able to love me back. And so, the conflict never occurs, the arguments never had, all sacrificed to the altar of comfort.

*

The concept of "comfort zones," the state in which we feel in control, calm, and sated, also comes to us from a biometeorological index. Originally coined in the 1920s as a descriptor of temperature, possibly as a marketing ploy, the comfort zone remains between 73 and 81 degrees Fahrenheit until it is claimed by metaphor in the 1970s. The use of "comfort zone" has continued to increase, with no sign of reaching its upper limit.

*

The problem with discomfort is that it does not annihilate us, not truly. Sitting frozen while a performer licked my mouth in that Vegas strip club, I only wished my discomfort would render me to nothing. But discomfort only pushes us out of our comfort zones for a moment, lighting up our boundaries so that we can see the oasis in which we spend most of our time.

Our comfort zones are not yet demilitarized.

If annihilation reduces us to nothing, discomfort reduces us to exactly the size of ourselves: a woman in a crowd unable to find the hands grabbing her, a punter in a strip club smug in her difference, a cipher in a man's myth. The size of ourselves, refusing to look beyond our own limit.

THE DOUBLE KING

Once, there were two kings inside one body, but there was no two-headed king. The double king had many daughters, and they grew, and many of them left the small green kingdom for small green kingdoms nearby. When only the youngest daughter remained, the double king busied himself with song. In tending to his daughters, the double king had forgotten the songbirds, and so he returned to tending his first charges.

*

My first memory is wiggling in the grass as my father diligently planted one hundred Scots pines. Those saplings are now stalwart. As a child with crooked bangs—my father trimmed them with his own father's desk scissors—I would check on the pines' growth every morning as my father and I did our rounds of the farm. Each day, we would check the magpie traps, refill the water for the bait bird and feed it, reset the trap, and if success had been had, I would wait in the truck while my father quietly wrung the neck of the caught predator.

*

The double king cleared his kingdom of the black-and-white doomsayers as much as he could, and as the rhymes of *One for sorrow, Two for mirth, Three for a funeral, Four for a birth* died out, the smaller birds' song swelled across the land.

*

I came into my father's life late. He had already started to weather—bruises staying a little longer—and I've never known his hair other than gray. Which is to say: he already had a strong sense of self and a litany of well-honed stories that began, "And then he'd say, Phil, he'd say. . . ." I will never know the skins my father shed, like the snakes in the shit heap, in order to become the man that made me.

✻

For many years, the double king used only his first face: broad and ruddy-cheeked. When his eldest daughters were young, he used his first face. When his youngest daughters were born, he used his first face. As the many magpies lessened, only one remained. The magpie took no joy in the rich orchestra of hedgerow song nor in the pride of the double king as he tended his daughters and tended his songbirds. Cursing the double king, the magpie flew to his table and crowed a hex that settled over his house and the whole kingdom.

✻

A bird in the house means death in the family. Often, a bird in literature means the death of the story—the clichéd weight exploding the delicate bones that are being heaped with metaphor. But the truth is the week I went to Britain and saw the full force, not the slight slippages or running together of daughters' names, of my father's dementia, my childhood home was invaded with birds. The robin dipping in the kitchen, not an ominous sign. Then, the panicked swallow orbiting the light in my bedroom. I threw a towel at it, waved a book, tried to be an air traffic controller and not flinch from its bullet body, and finally, it dropped behind a decrepit rocking horse. Grabbing the swallow and slipping it out of the window, I found its kin: three dead bird bodies stuck between the panes.

✻

The magpie's hex hovered over the double king, sinking slowly deeper into him. His first face still greeted the kingdom most days. Though his gait slowed, the double king still surveyed his kingdom, even as he traversed only its gardens and not its forests. But his first face began to flicker. At first, these brief intermissions were only glimpses of a second face: still broad but flat and colorless, as emphatic as a dishrag. This second face was empty but couldn't hold a thing: names, questions, and memories trickled out of it and wasted away.

✳

The question of "when?" is a weighted one when growing up with an older parent. When did they become old? My dad wasn't old at seventy, when he took joy in the two of us going to Sunday lunch alone and reveling in the awkward reactions of the servers when he corrected them: "No, my daughter, not my granddaughter." He wasn't old at my graduation, when with tears in his eyes at seeing the first of his family gain a degree, he slipped out of the hall so that he could hug me when the doe-eyed new graduates processed out into the world. Was he old when I flew home from America at twenty-two and he greeted me at Heathrow with a cardboard sign and a flask of gin? Does he remember when he became old? Does he remember anything?

✳

As the double king's second face emerged and settled, he began to stare at the kingdom instead of see it. The fields were still green, but the swaying corn did not move his eyes. He walked, slower now, in the gardens of the kingdom, but it was quiet. The songbirds did not recognize the double king's second face and so would not sing.

✳

On Mother's Day just gone, I mothered my father. Woke him up with tea and toast, hesitantly tucking his morning pills onto his plate, too. I sat with him, and we looped through the same questions, like a child unhappy with your answer to "why?," but the poke to repeat the question, the why before his "why?," would fly away before he could grasp it. I was only visiting for a week. Late in the afternoon the day before I was to leave, my father looked up from his deep blank silence and asked if I could cut his toenails. Because I don't live in this house anymore, I couldn't find any other scissors but the hulking ones his own father had owned, the scissors that my dad insisted on using to cut my hair until I was ten and old enough to go to his barber. I was as careful as I was taught to be.

*

One day, the double king ventured a little further than the garden but not quite to the forest. In the field lay a wooden contraption. Boxlike and weatherworn. The double king searched the box for meaning but found none. His second face blankly eyed the box's door as it swung open, closed. He did not remember the magpie trap, nor the songbirds. From the trees, the magpie who had cursed him cawed in victory.

*

Arriving home after that last visit, I dropped my suitcase in the kitchen, and leaving the door open, went to water the herbs outside. I made this small garden of green sprigs in pots when my father first started to fade away, a small way to feel close to him, the farmer. Returning inside there was a sparrow on the floor. Some curse followed me home. Calling my parents to assure them of a safe flight, my dad asks, "Where are you now?" and I mirror the question back to him, quietly, though he has already forgotten what I asked.

WHAT I SHOULD CONSIDER
BEFORE WEEPING IN FRUSTRATION
AT AIRLINE CUSTOMER SERVICE AFTER
A SIX-HOUR DELAY ON
MY HONEYMOON

1. I don't cry. No, really, I don't. At least, not identifiably—not outside, not in the world where someone might see or worse, remember.

2. Of course, there are tears of a kind. Basal tears are the fundamental lubricant of the eye, reflex tears react to irritants—I remember getting my nose pierced at sixteen, in a tent in a muddy music festival field, and being so indignant that my eyes sprang tears without my feeling pain. I've recognized that same look on the faces of amateur boxers getting punched in the ring, not in the safety of the gym, for the first time. A bodily betrayal.

3. The third and final tear type, the most mysterious, are those we sob.

4. The famous, or infamous, British "stiff upper lip" is a peculiarity of late nineteenth- into mid-twentieth-century Britain. We were a weepy nation before and would be again—but the emergence of empire in the Victorian era hardened the delicate sensibilities of Britain. The young queen at her coronation wept. With what? Tears of joy or fear, sorrow or bewilderment? But big empires don't cry. As the new century dawned, Britain dried her eyes and stoically marched on.

5. The mystery of emotional tears is a miracle to some: the act of weeping is often associated with Aristotle's idea of catharsis. Catharsis proposes an alchemy of sorts, with *Oedipus Rex* or your own choice of tearjerker as the catalyst: let art transform you. Spectating tragic art purges negative feelings—or, more plainly, "better out than in." Such a cliché holds a quieter threat: what will happen if you don't let it out? You'll curdle and rot.

6. The term *stiff upper lip* is actually an Americanism. The expression was treated with the suspicion of scare quotes throughout the nineteenth century.

7. My favorite mystic, Margery Kempe, never became a saint. I like to think that even for the Catholic Church, her endless tears—a gift from God—were too much. One traveling preacher went so far as to ban the tearful Margery from his sermon because he could not stand the disruption. What to do with a woman who won't shut up?

8. Historian of emotion Thomas Dixon situates Britain's suspicion of crying in a cat's cradle of paradoxes: the actor's paradox and the witch's paradox. For the actor—and we are all performers when we begin to weep—the contradiction lies in conveying authenticity as a professional faker. For the witch, it's a classic question of femininity: to weep is weak or manipulative, to remain dry-eyed is hard-hearted, unfeminine, bitch.

9. "Modern girls don't cry, even if they feel like it"—actress and World War I performer Dorothy Brunton.

10. I was deluged by Margery Kempe's tears in order to avoid the cathartic extremity of tragedy. As an undergraduate, I wanted to avoid the popular Shakespeare and Tragedy class, choosing instead the poker-faced sounding Literature and Law in Early Modern England. Beyond my discomfort at the prospect of three whole months of Elizabethan tearjerkers, an entire semester of Shakespeare at my medieval, top-tier university threatened to reveal my shameful lack of learning. I was a first-generation student, and it would take another degree or two to shake the feeling of not belonging, of intruding in someone else's sacred space—and so I would be as silent and small as I could in seminars. I forsook catharsis, focusing instead on the melding of English common law and social norms, and literature's role in scripting both.

11. A much cited 2011 study in *Science* found that women's tears contain chemical signals that decrease testosterone and sexual arousal in men. One of the study's authors, Noam Sobel, lamented, "I won't pretend to be surprised that it generated all the wrong headlines."

12. One of my oldest friends, Kit, can remember almost anything. They are the keeper of our archive. Kit remembers what I've worn for every Halloween since college. They recall the nasty specifics of fights with boyfriends I've long since forgotten. They remember that one-shouldered bronze dress I donated to Goodwill five years ago, which according to

them, was a mistake. But they do not remember ever having seen me cry. In over a decade of friendship, the most Kit can reach for is me sniffling on the phone and denying it.

13. Winston Churchill, that epitome of dry-eyed, bulldog Britishness, wept publicly during his tenure as prime minister—in the blitzed streets of London, in the House of Commons.

14. I used to think this was my fascination with Margery Kempe: a woman so loud in her life that she wrote the first autobiography in English, so she could echo down centuries. But now I wonder if my fascination comes down to the bafflement of opposites attracting. I'm stubbornly terrified of tears—at least tears that might be witnessed by another soul, but Margery did not fear them. Margery's tears stopped for no one, no matter how uncomfortable her audience.

15. News of weeping statues is a fairly regular miracle cycle. While condensation is often the culprit, there are weeping Madonna craft tutorials for all ages available online.

16. A smattering of smirking headlines stretching from 2013 to the present report on the establishment of "crying clubs." Human interest articles from Japan, England, and India report communal gatherings from ironic goth club nights to faceless conference room meetings all chasing the cathartic release of crying—but without the misery of loneliness. These gatherings, such as the Minnade Nako Kai in Kyoto and the Lachrymal Gland Club in Sendai, are seemingly particularly popular in Japan, ranked in the International Study on Adult Crying as among the most reserved nations in terms of public weeping.

17. The Northern Irish poet Seamus Heaney once described his relationship to Catholicism as less a religious practice and more tradition: "the specifically Irish Catholic blueprint that was laid down when I was growing up has been laid there forever. I think of the distrust of the world, if you like, the distrust of happiness, the deep pleasure there is in a mournful litany, the sense that there's some kind of feminine intercession that you turn to for comfort." I believe, too, that despite having lived in the United States for almost a decade, somewhere under the layers of my twisted transatlantic accent, adoption of Southernisms such as *y'all* but refusal to drop the

u from *colour*, is a Church of England blueprint etched in my soul—work hard, be polite, don't cry, and certainly don't let that lip wobble if someone can see you. The private vault of Protestant practice.

18. Why are Roy Lichtenstein's women crying? His crying girls are the most iconic faces of pop art. I still see their faces most days, repurposed in Atlanta street artist Chris Veal's murals across the city. The gesture remains static—cartoonishly beautiful women weep. In Lichtenstein's originals, blondes cry waiting for an absent man, sob out apologies, or bawl rather than ask for help, as in his famous *Drowning Girl*. In the Atlanta reimaginings, the telltale speech bubbles express similarly vapid stimuli for the women's tears: traffic, a dead iPhone battery, Instagram likes. The appeal of pop art is its immediacy of subject—we recognize the can of soup, the cartoon, and get to smugly nod in agreement with the ham-fisted critique of mass production, of low culture. That feeling of superiority buoys us for a brief moment. Lichtenstein's weeping women puff us up—we would never be so insipid as to cry over unworthy subjects.

19. My year of public crying: Oxford, 2011 to 2012. Angry at my own misery, I didn't care who saw me. I cried after classes. I cried on the Bridge of Sighs, I cried on Turl Street while walking past undergraduates throwing water balloons for a medieval rivalry, I cried on the bus to Oxford and away from it. I cried in tourist pictures. I cried in libraries full of priceless artifacts. I cried in the famous pubs and I cried in the student dives. I cried until I unceremoniously left—no graduation day, just a diploma in the mail. And then I stopped. In that medieval city, I was, briefly, Margery Kempe's daughter—weeping my ceaseless stream—a personal miracle of public emoting.

20. Tears lurk in the liminal spaces. The dark cinema is a British favorite in-between—the shadows obscuring both our tears and the line between fact and fiction, whether we are crying for the sentimental story onscreen or for ourselves.

21. On why there are so many weeping women in his work, Roy Lichtenstein shrugs: "Crying women are just the cliché. That's what you used to see in comics books—women who were like that, women were always in trouble."

22. *Maudlin,* meaning excessively sentimental or mawkish or foolishly emotional, comes from *Magdalene,* as in Mary Magdalene weeping, that most Catholic of icons.

23. Empire and antiweeping sentiment are a classic English couple. The dry-eyed English reserve is built on a misguided and murderous belief in the "better than." Better than those primitive, emotional "savages." Better than those Catholics crying in church. Better than those crying for their dead, the dead her majesty's men have made.

24. Weeping can be a weapon. The tears of white women, especially, are wont to be weaponized and brandished in defense of white supremacy. The tears of white women have called the cops, have made false accusations, have murdered people of color, and all the while maintain the sympathetic subject position.

25. The question of who gets to cry, rather than who wants to cry, weights our tears with the gravity the world affords us.

26. Letty Eisenhauer, Roy Lichtenstein's ex-lover with whom he lived when he first developed his mature pop art style, after he separated from his first wife, Isabel: "The crying girls are what he wanted women to be. He wanted to make you cry, and he did—he made me cry."

27. In his 2008 study on gender and affective behaviors, psychologist Jacob M. Vigil expressed surprise at the result that only 2 percent of American men reportedly believed they were likely to cry out of anger, as opposed to 51 percent of women. Vigil postulates this difference is linked to the social permissibility of men's, but not women's, aggression.

28. For all the reasons Margery Kempe and her spiritual advisors assign her holy tears—experiencing the suffering of Christ on the cross, seeing a wedding that reminds her of Mary and Joseph, seeing children and so imagining Christ as a child, recalling all of these spiritual insights for a scribe—anger is not one of them. She is mocked, accused of demonic possession, and endures the birth of fourteen children (not counting stillbirths) without modern pain medicine. Perhaps Margery wailed because it was her only outlet for rage.

29. After the Trump administration's brutal policy of family separation saw infants incarcerated in an old Walmart building, protesters gathered

outside the home of Homeland Security Secretary Kirstjen Nielsen. Instead of chanting protests, those gathered played audio recordings of the weeping migrant children.

30. My father repeatedly told me, "Don't marry a man you haven't seen cry."

31. Less than a year after I first met my husband in Atlanta, my visa ran out and I moved back to England, and so we broke up. It was not a surprising end. We weren't to know we had a decent shot at a sequel. What was surprising was the intensity of our bodies in our final week together, so much so that paths came together and blurred, and my tears prompted his erections. The joke that the reason I don't cry is because it arouses him has never died.

32. "Emotional incontinence" was and is the charge leveled at public outpourings of tears in Britain. This indictment leaks into the opinion pages whether the tears come after the death of Princess Diana or an underdog victory in the Premier League.

33. Scottish crime-fiction writer Ian Rankin positions his famous Detective John Rebus, mourning the death of his mentor, as paragon of national paradox: "Typical Scot, he couldn't cry about it. Crying was for football defeats, animal bravery stories, 'Flower of Scotland' after closing time."

34. In 2016, a farmer in rural China took to the media to complain that the medical system refused to believe his wife's condition: she had been crying stones for seven years.

35. Many of the more contemporary weeping miracles have been quickly demystified. Case in point: in 1996 a twelve-year-old Lebanese girl wept crystal tears. The sparkling tears were, in fact, quartz—as many as seven stones a day, for several months. With their sharpness, these tears brought blood, too. With the cameras and the headlines came skepticism, and it was quickly revealed that the crystalline tears were a scam, not a sacrament—a scheme of this poor girl's mother. She wanted her daughter to be seen, but the quartz tears only obscured, not amplified, the poor child's face.

36. It is only after I turn thirty that I tell anyone my most embarrassing secret: my mother has never said "I love you." I have seen her cry though, just once, when her dog was stuck underneath a hay bale.

37. Crying, like laughter, is one of the curious behaviors that separate us from animals—but does it elevate us?

38. The same year I start letting slip my maternal secrets, I finally get fitted for contact lenses—as if I can escape charges of vanity now that my twenties are behind me. Secreting until my eyes were red with the practice of scooping the circle of plastic in and out, I ask my optometrist if he thinks it is beneficial to cry. "You aren't crying," he says, "your body is just protecting you from yourself."

VACATION

The refrain leaks over and over the candy-colored synchronized waterskiing: "Vacation, all I ever wanted. / Vacation, had to get away. / Vacation, meant to be spent alone." This is the Go-Go's 1982 video for their single "Vacation." Tiaras and pearls and tutus and giggling. The splashing is palpable. A 1950s teenage dream of kitsch that Katy Perry is still singing.

From the opening shot, Belinda Carlisle guides the pile of white women, sullen in their magazine flipping, to the promised land, vacation. Not saved by a white knight, but instead given the freedom of their own tomorrow: *Tomorrow's a day of mine that you won't be in.*

Perhaps you were not alive in 1982.

Perhaps you wrote off the Go-Go's as a girl band, "ugly punklings turned America's sweetheart" in one contemporaneous reviewer's eyes.

Perhaps you have lived a life that never brought you near Belinda Carlisle's voice.

But perhaps you'd still recognize the song: it plays in the background of Michael Moore's *Fahrenheit 9/11* as George W. Bush golfs prior to the 9/11 attacks. It soundtracks car commercials, it is montage music for countless sitcoms, it is covered in *Glee*: whenever you need the carefree sense of summer's good clean fun, there it is.

Vacation, all I ever wanted. Vacation, had to get away. Vacation, meant to be spent alone.

*

The personal is political.

To vacate: freedom from obligations, leisure, release. The personal is political, unless, for a time, we have the leisure of vacating from our person. I do. I can vacate whenever I want.

*

We are in Minneapolis, the Walker Art Center. A welcome, if brief, vacation.

I sit in front of Joan Mitchell's *Hemlock* (1954) for fifteen minutes. I get up, leave the white room, and mistake myself. I come back. This occurs three times.

Later, outside, the steel skies draw me back to Joan Mitchell's exploding deep green and white. *Hemlock* (1954) is clearly not one of Mitchell's more famous canvases—and later proves impossible to find in facsimile, all Googling showing the painting to be overtaken by *Hemlock* (1956). But this earlier *Hemlock* is, for a few minutes, mine.

I know that another person's recollection of a painting is almost as boring as listening to a friend recall their dream from last night, but hear me out. I can't tell you to Google it. Centered in a vast white block, what looks like a black hood unbillowing reveals on repeated looking to be greens emerging with darkness from the canvas. Some blue emerges, a breath of gray. The ocher emerges most slowly.

As the color moves like smoke up out of the canvas, I exhale deeply. I forget the academic struggles awaiting my return. I forget the twenty-four people killed in a bus accident in Bangladesh, the three people shot and murdered in a Milan courtroom. I exhale; so deeply my shoulders drop.

I forget.

*

What I forget is what I have vacated.

In graduate school, my closest friend, Zoe, was the only black woman in a program of sixty-six people. Our supposedly liberal faculty of fiction writers and poets repeatedly ignored her experiences of racism, labeling her an angry black woman who "hated white people" and "hated men." Perversely, a white female professor told us that the voice of Rodney King was speaking through her and telling us that these student complaints must be deescalated. Read: quiet down.

When hundreds of students (predominantly white) signed a letter of solidarity with Zoe, note was taken. The terms *libel* and *slander* were sent by the head of the department to explain Zoe's description of her experiences. Those who offered solidarity with Zoe, who shared her story and their eyewitness accounts of these events, were told that their speaking out was "cyberbullying" against the white man and the tenured faculty whose behavior was in question. Repeated legal threats were made against Zoe and her supporters, all for questioning the behavior of an institution that named its library after W. E. B. Du Bois and seemingly decided that that was enough.

Protections were given to the white man who sexually and verbally harassed Zoe. To the white man who told her she could have gotten into any prestigious graduate writing program because she had "that whole Junot Díaz thing going." To the white man who said he would never want to be in a workshop with her because she wrote about black people. The same man, who after months of publicly disdaining and belittling her, aggressively licked her mouth while she tried to escape him.

As I write this, in my white safety, no action other than the natural course of our graduation has been taken. The university beyond our department is currently being investigated for Title IX violations.

Besides Zoe and me, two other white women, women who loved her and wanted to love our community, became similar targets of downcast eyes in the university's hallways. We were all passed over for teaching positions and fellowships. Zoe, Molly, and another Caroline were no longer welcome in workshop. The professor who had ventriloquized Rodney King dropped me from her class because she'd gathered from Twitter that I was a feminist and might find the class "troubling." Molly was so unwelcome that she lost a year, graduating early to escape the celebrated writing program.

We became the wicked witches of western Massachusetts. The cackling wenches best avoided, better heckled.

*

And when I am tired, I can return to the safety of blank white canvas. Before the ocher emerges. Before it complicates.

What have I even learned about my whiteness?

Not all white women who identify as feminists are white feminists. Not all white feminists are white. But white feminism is largely made by white women for white women, who consider the average woman, the universal female, to be straight, cis, and white. Women who look like me.

We celebrate the Nineteenth Amendment of 1920—finally women's right to vote—on August 26. We name it Women's Equality Day. Google makes doodles for it. Perhaps there are parades. But due to widespread voter suppression for decades more, this does not mark the beginning of suffrage for women of color. The conflation of *women* with *white women* conveniently smooths the narrative.

Wherever we stand politically, we are most likely to recognize the seventy-seven cents to a dollar statistic of the gender wage gap. Again, the conflation of *women* with *white women*: black women make sixty-four cents to the white male dollar, Hispanic and Latinx women fifty-four cents.

Joan Mitchell: "I don't want to look at descriptions of horror. I mean, the world's horrible but do I have to hang it on my wall?" Though she uttered this offhand statement before Twitter, this may as well have been hashtagged #whitefeminism.

The safety of a blank white canvas.

I have been a white feminist. My women's history was Boudicca, Elizabeth I, Mary Wollstonecraft, Emmeline Pankhurst, and the contraceptive pill. Judy Chicago's *The Dinner Party* when my eyes got really widened. It is not difficult to see this light is scoldingly, blindingly, white.

And likely I will fall to white feminism again. I will forget the value of my seventy-seven cents.

I will forget that American Indian women experience sexual assault at almost twice the national average. I will forget that the contraceptive pill came at the price of Puerto Rican women's forced sterilization. I will forget that African American women experience intimate partner violence at a rate 35 percent higher than white women.

I will forget.

∗

Moving on from Joan Mitchell, begrudgingly, I encounter one of the Walker's treasures: Yves Klein's *Suaire de Mondo Cane (Mondo Cane Shroud)*. The large canvas showcases his signature blue, daubed to the fabric with "living brushes," the bodies of women loaded up with paint and released under his instruction.

I take a picture and address it: "A woman's body is only a tool so I fucked up your precious blue with my Instagram filter, Yves Klein." I do not even think twice about reconstructing color to fit my own narrative.

*

Above my desk in Massachusetts is an old Union flag my sister gave me, its red, white, and blue pleasantly faded. Above Zoe's desk is a beaten up baroque gold-framed blackboard with Junot Díaz chalked in: "Who told these people we were safe?"

She crafted this in the year we lived together. We made many things. We fed each other with the products of our hands. Though the house's sacred place should have been our writing desks, our church was the kitchen. I still own the outrageously large skillet, the one that needed two burners, we bought for steaks. As if we could afford steak.

Two years later, Zoe, Caroline, and I attend a reading by Claudia Rankine. She reads from *Citizen*. I have dragged Zoe (a fiction writer) to enough poetry readings that I have a gross tumor of pride for finally attending together a poet that reflects her in a mirror. My gold star.

The only note I have from those hours: "Comfort at any price is not comfort at all." As if my comfort weren't a more affordable commodity.

*

The week before Zoe and I leave Massachusetts for good she asks me to dye her hair, an act she has been performing on my stubbornly red hair for several months.

"You're the first white girl to dye my hair."

She cackles: Zoe never just laughs.

I'm scared of messing up. She talks me through it—it feels good to be making things together again.

We plan food for the Harry Potter party she's throwing: I promise stodgy British dishes, she's making pretzels. Later the photos will show the four of us, Zoe, Molly, Caroline, and I, doused in black gowns and smiling a little too hard. Smiling, as if to play the part of witches so well that we might soon, finally, get a touch of power.

I'm leeching out pigment. It works. By the time we've rinsed out each other's hair in the kitchen sink, the floor is soaked and we're both blonder.

Because Zoe loves me, she makes kind jokes when the woman who looks like me waits, freezing, outside the freestanding Bank of America kiosk, instead of inside like usual, because a young black man is currently withdrawing cash.

"It's so great that racism is over in Massachusetts!"

Because she loves me, I'm too ashamed to say sorry.

I'm telling you this because I have hurt what I love with my vacations. Any allyship is a recognition of rupture, of uncrossable gulf. What is necessary is committing to continual staring at your failure, your deficit, and continuing to build the bridge you know will make it only halfway across.

✳

Vacation is a middle-class institution. Replacing the British notion of holidays (easily traced back to *holy days*), the American vacation is very literally born of the idea of removing and recapturing oneself. When the most luxurious of New York City's travelers (the Vanderbilts, the Rockefellers, the Carnegies) began to declare they would "vacate" their city lives for upstate lakeside pleasures, "vacation" overtook the British "holiday."

The middle classes followed suit, the mid-nineteenth-century rush of the Adirondacks stampeding language itself.

Though I am British and not a Rockefeller, I have spent periods of summer in the Adirondacks more than once. *Vacation, all I ever wanted. Vacation, had to get away.*

When Zoe visits the lake for a weekend, she is armed with notebooks, "Gotta do my novel research on white people." And then we sliver a dozen onions to caramelize for grilled cheese sandwiches.

✳

In discussing her allegiance to abstract expressionism, Joan Mitchell conjures the specter of her father. The figure disappears from her work because "he couldn't even criticize what it was." And with that stride into abstraction, she "felt protected. That I remember so clearly."

It is not so unusual to employ abstraction as protection. I've seen the institution, the socialization, the family upbringing to shroud the instant repulsions, the snakes inside the chest, the thoughts given dollar words to sound something fancier than *you're less.*

I've looked in the mirror, too. The convenient fog of *but I'm not the problem,* the cobweb of complicity so finely wrought as to be barely felt on my skin.

✳

The day before I leave for Minneapolis, I engage in group sex with my partner and a younger woman. She has a name you wouldn't believe in this context, and that concludes my knowledge of her beyond her tan lines. Afterward, my partner will joke that I became a field marshal in directing these bodies to stage my desires.

When I encounter Yves Klein's *Suaire de Mondo Cane* four days later, I will not consider the vacation I took from a strident feminism that rails against sexual objectification of women. I will not question the "living brushes" I have used to achieve my own desires.

The value of leisure time is often depicted as a refilling of the depleted tumbler of self. A spiritual topping off. *Vacation, meant to be spent alone.*

A brief, selfish absence that brings you back fighting better, faster, stronger.

Am I a better ally for the nights I've retreated to sitcoms that reflect me out of exhaustion from "the fight"? Am I a more fortified feminist for my days off?

Of course not.

This is the central lie of white feminism, a feminism that bleaches everything back to the simpler white canvas. It is a feminism that promises those outside that we will clean our house, and when it's done, we'll invite everyone else in. Except the house is never ours to clean, to renovate.

A white feminism is not feminism at all. A white feminism advocates the extensions of certain male privileges, with no interest in equality. *You,* white woman, may get into an Ivy League school, but in return *you* will uphold masculine modes of academic excellence. *You,* white woman, can run for president, but in return *you* will uphold the system that orchestrates wage disparity. *You,* white woman, will be one of the guys, and *you* will not bite the hand that feeds you.

A high tide can raise all boats only if you keep your eyes heavenward to ignore those who are drowning.

*

It is not without some hope that we left Massachusetts. The four of us, the wicked witches of western Massachusetts, found each other. Before the many hours packing furniture into the New York–bound truck for Zoe, we had planned a cleansing. Not to forget but to tame the memory. We would burn sage, smoke out the rotten heart of what our graduate experience had become. We would dance and hug, cackle and hex. We would delight in the herb smoke, like, for a time, we could believe it wasn't already decided who would walk away unburned.

But we forgot those plans: it never happened; we were never cleansed.

THE ARSONISTS

If your ears are burning, you are the subject of heated conversation. Roman writers Plautus and Pliny the Elder both held that the right ear burns if you are being praised, the left ear burns for slander. Pliny would die in Pompeii, engulfed by the toxic gas emitted from Mount Vesuvius's fiery depths. Sometimes, we burn in surround sound. Sometimes, when my ears burn, I still think Lauren is asking someone if she was right to choose her husband over me.

Only women were burned for treason, men were hanged.

I burned sage along with Lauren's yearbook that somehow ended up at my parents' house. I saved my own yearbook from the flames—the thirty flimsy pages of photos and promises of friendship forever in Lauren's delicate cursive. The memories she described are as hazy as smoke now, in-jokes lost to high school detritus: my terrible driving, the sugar she still took in her tea. We used to burn each other mix CDs—the adolescent emo screamings of the boys I was dating exchanged for the classic rock and Fleetwood Mac of her dad's expansive record collection—and she never admonished me for lighting cigarette after cigarette.

She never got to see me quit.

We burned the distance of continents: when I was homesick in Massachusetts, in Georgia, in Scotland, I burned for her. When I scraped Marmite on blackened toast. When my father, losing his memory, still asked after

Lauren on my weekly phone calls—losing my husband's name, the name of the city I live in, but still grasping the name of the girl with the freckles who'd worn the same ugly green-and-yellow-kilted school uniform as me a decade previously.

In 2001, we entered our second year of high school while foot-and-mouth disease ran rampant through the farmland. For weeks, pyres of culled cows burned. I couldn't go home for fear of carrying the disease to further herds. Sometimes when I eat barbecue, the smell reminds me of those weeks living with Lauren as a sister.

In one of the stories collected by the Brothers Grimm, a straw, a coal, and a bean escape the fate of an old woman's fire and cooking plans. In the comradery of lucky escape, they travel far together, farther and farther until the merry band find themselves at a brook with no bridge. So that the friends may move forward, the straw lays herself down to form a bridge. The coal, being selfish, pushed ahead impetuously to walk over the water first, the bean following behind him. The straw burned. The coal fell and fizzled in the river. The bean fell but floated, finally drifting ashore, but had swallowed so much water that she burst. A tailor, passing by, took pity and sewed the bean back together. Whole, but mourning. The moral of the story is that no one escapes the fire unscathed. Perhaps that is the cost of friendship.

When Lauren's then-boyfriend now-husband flew in another woman to fuck for weeks while she visited me, I thought we would burn him in effigy. Visiting from England, Lauren was driving across the southern states with me—it was the furthest we'd lived apart.

Perhaps they burned effigies at their wedding, I wouldn't know.

I forget whether the bridge in Oxford, where Lauren fled to me after he finally admitted infidelity, is called the Bridge of Tears or the Bridge of Sighs. Either way, she burned it. It took two years for him to tell her the truth. She wasn't the first to know.

Her friends, our friends—high school comrades who had also made it to London from our rural nothing—had been unwitting accomplices and kept his secrets until they couldn't. I don't remember the exact match that struck, but someone told Lauren's twin brother, and the heat was on. More than anger, she melted with shame. Dripping red sheets of it. She stayed with me for a while, sleeping on the floor of my tiny apartment. The way I remember it she was weeping.

She built the bridge to go back to him and I burned it. Afterward he told me this was my fault, that I was a wedge between them, that my grief at holding the fragments of my best friend together was poisoning their re-union. He yelled and yelled at me, and Lauren told me she didn't know who to believe.

Burning the flag is either an act of desecration and protest or an act of retirement and respect.

In the four years after her now-husband's infidelity, our friendship slow-burned to cinder. Lauren told me I didn't respect her choice to go back to him. The year she married him, we tried. We tried to keep the ashes from scattering. He refused to see me. My presence hurt him too much. When I finally moved back to England the year Lauren married him, every apology I tried to utter burned my throat and came out as nothing more than smoke—the sorry for not trying harder, for not congratulating harder, for never faking it convincingly enough, as if she didn't know the twitching contours of my face as thoroughly as any map of her own countenance.

There's no shortage of writers who'd rather burn their lives than let go of their own story: Somerset Maugham made his secretary watch as he shoveled his letters into the fireplace; Eudora Welty considered her auto-biographical materials and concluded, "I think I'd better burn everything up"; Emily Dickinson instructed her sister, Lavinia, to burn all her papers upon her death; Franz Kafka asked a friend for the same. There are plenty of stories burned by the benevolent protection of others. Both Lord Byron and Lady Mary Wortley Montagu had their autobiographies burned by those intending to preserve their reputations. What arrogant saviors, to burn someone else's life.

Lauren burned me from her life's story so she would not have to remember her husband hot for someone else.

The year she married him was the only year since our rupture that we lived in the same city: London. After three years in the United States, I'd moved home to the United Kingdom, and we tried. We tried to reignite our friendship, but the cautious coffee dates and museum visits only made the coldness between us more apparent. I had to cross the river to see her. There are thirty-three bridges across the Thames. Once our bridge was burned, every high school friend remaining burned away. In a city so connected, I was a single, solitary flame.

In the Romantic period, to be *burned* was to be plagued by venereal disease. I want to be a better person, but I still hope his dick burns when he pisses.

The week before I left London to move back to the United States permanently, Lauren and I had dinner, and I knew then it was burned out. She was hurt I hadn't wished her a happy wedding day. I was still just hurt. Over scorching curries, our small talk was polite, cold.

Augustine believed purgatory was flames. *Ignis emendatorius,* "correctional fire." A kind of punishing passing place, where the human sin is burned out of us in order to move on. After I'd left the United Kingdom with my two suitcases, I celebrated Lauren's birthday by printing her wedding photos at Walgreens and burning them. Not correctional, but cleansing.

I burned the bridge and built another one to the city famous for burning. Atlanta's infamous blazing has been rebranded as the phoenix rising from the ashes—the city's motto is *Resurgens:* "Rise up." A second chance at something more beautiful. Moving back from London, I thought again of the memories we'd made here, how those memories no longer had a home.

When Lauren came to Atlanta years ago, we sat by a campfire while her now-husband fucked someone else. An American, it turns out. We stayed in Atlanta only a few nights, not long enough to take the tourist route to Martin Luther King's eternal flame or the monument to revival that is the iconic downtown sculpture *Atlanta from the Ashes*. She burned the bridge and I burned the bridge and I never thought to tell her about phoenixes.

BOYS ON THE RADIO

OK, so there's Orpheus, and the beasts lay down and the birds adore him and he actually seems like maybe, maybe an OK guy, doubting aside, but you have to ask exactly what happened when Eurydice followed him back from Hades, no question, if she really would have followed her husband if she'd known that thousands and millions of teenage girls and not so teenage women would keep following her path up toward the light, if she'd seen me following the creepy drummer, the emo guitarist, the good drummer, at least a few bassists, the amateur anythings to dingy bars, muddy fields, repurposed churches, and hotel lounges, would she, Eurydice, the very first groupie, have made an actual decision and stayed down there—think of the things Eurydice's eye-lined army of girls could have achieved if she'd stayed in hell: a presidency, a sales tax system that refunds tampons, tampons that don't smell like the perfumed closet drawers of some aunt's house, maybe just free tampons, a fourth Bikini Kill album, an actual verifiable reason for "fat-free" to mean "cardboard-tasting," condoms that don't feel impossibly cold when trashing them, a fourth Tuscadero reunion, any Helium reunion, a better version of the speculum, a cure for endometritis, a cure for the wage gap, a cure for love songs in which the girl is coy and that's a crisis; think of the things *I* could've achieved: unmarred lungs, extra credit, any musical skill of my own, a better résumé, a better dating résumé, a working knowledge of how income tax actually works, more income, a less selfish approach to volunteering, teeth to make an American dentist proud, fewer face holes: staying in hell and getting shit done—isn't that more punk than sneaking into gigs when you're a kid and dating an older guy, when in fact you aren't the one moving anywhere, your body is being dragged down into a pit where you don't question why a fifteen-year-old in fishnets isn't ID'd at the bar or why an almost thirty-year-old man is dating a fifteen-year-old and nobody mentions the word statutory or thinks to gently take you aside in the dank basement club bathroom where the toilet doors are long gone but that scratched out graffiti has been layering phone numbers on the wall since the eighties and say *Honey, let's talk*, and sure the fifteen-year-old in the fishnets would probably have eye-rolled like that one girl I saw at a show years later, when I'd given up kohl completely, maybe she was sixteen and maybe she did look like a younger me, but even so I could see her and I could see the drinks she didn't buy at the bar and I could see who was buying them and his sleight of hand not fooling even your shittiest mall magician, and when I put my hand on her shoulder, she shrugged with an eye roll that could've triggered an avalanche, and it crushed me, which is all to say that Eurydice might not have saved us if she'd said fuck it, said anything and stayed back in hell, but Eurydice, girl, hell might've let us play our own songs.

UNION

My husband shares a first name with Cyrus West Field, the entrepreneur behind the first transatlantic submarine telegraph. A man who shrank the world, collapsing two thousand miles of ocean from a ten-day ship voyage to mere minutes.

Coincidence can often lure us into fate, or at least a belief in the thread of connection—the story waiting to be told.

The transatlantic submarine telegraph was an act of both incredible invention and staggering arrogance. Much like a marriage.

Cyrus West Field had no oceanography experience. No engineering experience, either. What he did have was a rich network and confidence bordering on hubris. Under his Atlantic Telegraph Company, he finagled financial backing from both the British and American governments, as well as other private investors. The project began in 1854, a mere sixteen years after working telegraph technology was introduced to the world. Ships from both sides of the ocean sailed toward each other, the cable was pitched off the back and left to sink to unknown depths. Four years later, the project was complete. Cyrus West Field had conquered the Atlantic.

On August 16, 1858, the first official message conveyed congratulations from the company's British directors to their American counterparts. Floodgates open, the cavalcade of celebratory messages began. Queen Victoria telegrammed President James Buchanan: "The Queen is convinced that the President will join her in fervently hoping that the electric cable, which now connects Great Britain with the United States, will prove an additional link between the nations, whose friendship is founded upon their common interest and reciprocal esteem. The Queen has much pleasure in thus communicating with the President and renewing to him her wishes for the prosperity of the United States."

The president responded with even greater fervor: "The President cordially reciprocates the congratulations of her majesty the Queen on the success of the great international enterprise accomplished by the science, skill, and indomitable energy of the two countries.

"It is a triumph more glorious, because far more useful to mankind, than was ever won by conquer on the field of battle.

"May the Atlantic telegraph, under the blessing of Heaven, prove to be a bond of perpetual peace and friendship between the kindred nations, and an instrument destined by Divine Providence to diffuse religion, civilization, liberty and law throughout the world."

∗

It was over in three weeks. The cable frayed, communication faltered, complete failure. The man who shares my husband's name was not deterred: Cyrus West Field simply started again.

The relationship that would become my marriage also had a false start. Faced with an Atlantic distance between us as my student visa came to an end, we cut the cord after a few months of dating.

∗

Another coincidence of naming: one of the ships involved in laying the replacement cable was the ss *Caroline*.

∗

I moved back to the United States barely a year after our initial breakup, and though he was in Georgia and I was in Massachusetts, we were young and still heartbroken, and well, you know the story.

My short author bio used to contain the sentence "She lives between Old England and New England." In the three years I lived in Massachusetts, I never stopped being struck by a mixture of confusion, amazement, and horror at running into place-names that I'd grown up with in England. The capital of my small Celtic county is a Cape Cod vacation town. Plymouth, the city where I was born, is reimagined as a more insidious origin story at Plymouth Rock. The betweenness of that history.

I could speculate that I am not the first of my family to be transatlantic. If I could ever accept the strangeness of being married and accept myself as a part of a new family, then I wouldn't need speculation. My husband's family mythos paints their origins all over Europe. The betting is Irish or Scottish, with an outside chance of German. It's a rigged bet, though, already won: they are white Americans, born citizens.

I met my husband two weeks after I came to the United States for the first time on a short-term fellowship. I did not know at twenty-two, drunk on lust for newness, that I would eventually call this man and this country home. More importantly, I knew nothing of the systems and mazes of bureaucracy I would have to shout this naming into, the stacks of papers that would contort this love into dry, officious promises.

As a Brit in America much small talk with strangers revolves around my rapidly fading accent. In Lyft rides, in post office lines, at the grocery store, the routine dance of "Where you from?" begins. It is a seemingly innocuous question that since the 2016 election has curdled to become insidious. If the questioner is white, there are a limited number of outcomes that range from polite to abhorrent, all offered in the same tone of well-mannered stranger:

1. The questioner asks for geographic specificity, despite my coming from a farm in a tiny and insular county, where nothing ever happens but sheep.
2. The questioner responds to my answer that I'm from Britain but I've lived in the United States for a considerable chunk of my adult life with a cheery "Me too!" Of course, in this situation the stranger means their ancestors were British, and I continue to find these claims irritating.
3. With little to no context about my visa or employment history, the questioner congratulates me on getting here "the right way."

The first time this third outcome occurred, in a Lyft on the way to the airport to visit my family back in Britain, I was genuinely confused. In the repetitions of this scenario in the years since, I remember that initial confusion with nostalgia. I still play confused when this script repeats every few months—I will ask the polite stranger what "the right way" is, and without fail, the right way is a vague explanation of "through the right channels, legal. . . ."

That I was shocked at the audacity of other white people to express anti-immigrant xenophobia while praising my own immigration I now find precious.

This stranger small talk usually ends with my brief spiel about the costs and struggles of immigration—even my own, which is the "right way." The "right way" is the story white people tell themselves. The story that anyone who looks like them must have a right to live here. Though I have worked for state institutions for many years, taught your children, paid my taxes, my immigration is a cheat—I got married. It's the easy way. No doubt easier as a white woman—the questions more gentle, the eye contact less accusatory, my cultural difference considered cute, not contemptuous.

The easy way looks like this: Several thousand dollars for an immigration lawyer to prepare the application. Hundreds and hundreds and hundreds of pages including: every address, every tax return, every lease. Your marriage certificate. Wedding photos. Photos from any significant occasion. Vacation itineraries. Plane tickets. Letters. Emails. Birthday cards from when you were broken up that you probably shouldn't have kept. Engagement announcements. All your bank accounts. Car insurance. Dental insurance. Anything with a dollar sign and both your names. A five-hundred-dollar physical examination from a government-approved doctor. Biometrics: another hundred bucks for the privilege of being fingerprinted and photographed—again. Another five hundred dollars to file the application.

And then you sit still and wait.

You'll be called for an interview. You will not be together. The questions will range from "How did you meet?" to a request for a diagram of the marital bedroom. You will tell the officer your love story. It should be clear, crafted, and authentically accurate. Your story must convince the officer, who sees thousands of couples every year, that romance is real.

∗

Stories are slippery, shapeshifting depending on the audience.

My marriage can be packaged into saccharine romance. It's a transatlantic rom-com! A love story across an ocean! A wish-fulfillment wet dream!

The truth is, I love my husband. The truth is, he planned exactly the wedding I wanted (steak and chips, and fifteen people). The truth is, if it weren't for the vagaries of immigration, we never would've married at all.

∗

Among her many honors, Queen Victoria is credited with establishing contemporary conventions of the white wedding. I wore black at my wedding, because I always wear black, but I did cave to a white lace skirt for the engagement celebration my parents insisting on having in a quaint British church.

My marriage remains Victorian. I imagine that Victoria, as the queen of England, was not bogged down in the slow-churning machine of immigration bureaucracy in her choice to marry Albert, a foreign national. But it is during her reign that British and U.S. law encoding gender and marriage to both a man and the state begin to flourish.

Much of U.S. marriage law was shipped over wholesale from English common law, including the concept of coverture. Coverture describes the status of a woman in marriage: under the cover of her husband. As a legal entity, the woman ceases to exist—she becomes the citizen of her husband.

The 1855 revision of the U.S. Naturalization Act explicitly identified the domain of citizenship as the domain of the husband. If a noncitizen woman married an American citizen, she was required to assume American citizenship. Such a ruling did not apply for men. It would be almost a century until women could petition on behalf of their spouse in 1952, and in that century a woman's citizenship remained precariously contingent on her performance as wife.

The 1907 U.S. Expatriation Act declared a woman who married an alien lost her citizenship. If her husband became a naturalized citizen, she could apply to regain citizenship through the naturalization process. While the Cable Act, also known as the Married Women's Independent Nationality Act, seemingly corrected this law in 1922, it left enough cracks for coverture's influence to still be felt.

When I asked my husband to marry me, I asked him to cover me with his U.S. citizenship.

*

The peculiarity of immigration law's language is inescapable. I have been an "alien" for almost a decade. One day, I will be "natural" by virtue of marriage. This narrative of a woman's body as monstrous but made normal by matrimony is a familiar one.

All stories are snakes.

To the Victorian public, the transatlantic submarine telegraph was the eighth wonder of the world and a triumph of humanity's need to communicate. To Cyrus West Field, the telegraph was an investment opportunity that offered him the role of protagonist.

Hans Christian Andersen tells his own story of the telegraph cable in "The Great Sea-Serpent." The "new wonder story" follows a little fish "of good family" as he swims through the chaos caused by the arrival of the cable —"a long heavy thing that looked as if it would never come to an end." In his search to find out what this monstrous interloper to the seafloor is, the little fish encounters whales and sharks and sawfish, who are turned from predators to coinvestigators by the mystery of the cable. The sea dwellers determine it is a great sea serpent, a mighty eel, until finally a sea cow enlightens them as to the human origin of the mechanism. The little fish still believes the hulking snake must be something more magical, and he's right: the cable *is* more magical—it thinks and listens to the surrounding sea creatures, all the while crackling with the sparks of human communiqués. The cable is silent, because it can be: "So it gave no answer; it had something else to attend to; it telegraphed and lay in its lawful place."

"The Great Sea-Serpent" is a truly mediocre fairy tale. But it tells the story of technological awe, extreme phallic hubris, and the depths to which the entitlement of white Europeans can sink under the guise of exploration.

*

Other white people, when they don't congratulate me on immigrating "the right way," occasionally express genuine surprise that a British person needs a visa in order to live in the United States. I used to repeat this as a joke—all that wasted tea. It's a weak punch line, one that falls apart with minimal pressure from self-examination.

This story is funny because it's true. It's the blither side of the coin to the false narrative of "the right way"—but it's the same story, a story that begins by eating its own tail.

*

When we tell stories enough, they become archetypes: tragedies, romances, fairy tales.

As two people who were not particularly matrimonially inclined, my husband and I have smoothed the edges of our engagement story with repeated tellings into the cold, hard pebble of a punch line: the romance of a proposal with both parties weeping in an immigration lawyer's parking lot.

It's a funny story. It's also highly truncated—we'd bobbed and weaved around the fact of our transatlanticism for seven years. That grand gulf that Cyrus West Field saw as a canvas on which to paint his entrepreneurial fame has haunted the relationship that ended up as my marriage, hanging between our birth certificates as our love's death warrant.

By the time we proposed—and we both tried to make up for the parking lot later with sweet gestures, me at the college campus where we first fell in love, him in the north Georgia mountains—marriage was the last resort. Not to save our relationship, but to save my right to live here.

*

I am still waiting to tell the government my love story. Current processing times are estimated at thirteen to thirty-three months. So I sit and wait—I cannot leave the country without abandoning my application.

This is the easy way.

I cannot imagine who might have it easier—being able to afford this process, alone, is an extreme privilege, as is the fact that my husband treats me with respect as I am now bureaucratically at his mercy. It's a good lesson in American life: the easy way is easy only if you can afford it.

*

I have been telling you one story of my marriage—the shape of narrative mapped onto the Atlantic. There are others.

I could've told you that I went to college with my husband's cousin, years before we ever met, or the other coincidences that have stacked up to a fate. I could've told you the true story of how I proposed, or how I'd read his mother's work on modernism as an undergraduate, or the many other strewn details of our lives that jigsaw together, each fit for a coo of *Oh you two were meant to be!*

There are better ways to tell a love story. There are better endings than a comfortable, bureaucratically beneficial marriage—and there are many more worse.

*

Stories can slip right out of sight—the illusion of ending. I have rewritten this attempt several times. I brought you in at the end of the journey when the travel has slowed to become simply a life.

There's no ending here: I will continue to be married and continue to wait for immigration approval based on that marriage. I will till death do us part or divorce, and what kind of narrative resolution do either of these options offer?

I will wait to be covered by my husband's citizenship, and until then I will be covered by my whiteness—a coverage that ensures I will continue to be read as resident, as she who should inherit this earth because America's white supremacy will continue.

The Atlantic will continue to host journeys as quotidian and meaningful as my own. Somewhere in that ocean's depths, the transatlantic telegraph cable hums its path for the hundreds of cables—telegraph, telephone, internet—that have been laid in the century and a half since

Cyrus West Field first instructed those cords of wire to be thrown off the back of the boat.

All endings are a deus ex machina. That's the problem with stories—they change shape until suddenly they disappear completely, all with someone declaring themselves the god behind the scenes.

The year I was born saw the first transatlantic fiber-optic cable laid—another revolution of transatlantic communications that enabled the American and European early internets to knit together. Another coincidence of fact that can be built to some idea of fate.

ORIGIN UNKNOWN

We think we are her only two daughters.

NAME:	Mother
BIRTH DATE:	June 6, 1945
BIRTHPLACE:	Unknown
FAMILY:	I remember visiting her father's house in Bath, once. He had just died. I was four or five. I don't know what my grandfather's first name was. I know I cherished a miniature penknife with a mother-of-pearl handle that I believe he gave me. But I don't have the memory to confirm.
OCCUPATION:	When I'm old enough to start remembering, my sister and I are my mother's job.

I realized my mother was a pathological liar before I got my first period. In the years before I left home, I made it into a game: How many can I catch in a week, in a day? How dumb will she go? Is she really going to claim she had not driven to the village shop for milk when I took my bike through the field shortcut and saw her at the checkout counter?

NAME:	Mother
BIRTH DATE:	June 6, 1945
BIRTHPLACE:	Unknown
FAMILY:	Her mother was called Frieda. I don't know exactly when she died, but it happened before I was born to my mother at forty-two. My mother has never uttered

this name. There's a walking stick in the hallway made of a cabbage stem with "Frieda" carved into it. I asked about it once, and that's the entirety of knowing my grandmother.

OCCUPATION: Once, my mother was a bank clerk in Chelsea. Then, it was housekeeper for a widowed aristocratic lady. Then, something with horses. Then, something in a pub. Then another story, then another, and another.

At six, I start a series of recurring dreams that will stay with me for twenty years: I don't know my mother's face. The one I recognize is a mask. The mask comes off at dinner, at school, at my wedding, in the grocery store, in London, in Paris, in the bathroom, at church, in the airport. When the mask comes off, the nightmare begins. I wake up again, still not knowing her face.

NAME: Mother
BIRTH DATE: June 6, 1945
BIRTHPLACE: Unknown
FAMILY: The formula is difficult. I've never met an aunt or an uncle, a cousin or niece or nephew, but I can't trust that my mother is an only child. My dad, with his slipping memory, asked me last Christmas if my mother had any family and I could only answer, "Not that I know of."
OCCUPATION: Perhaps she'd been a spy. A still unknown Soviet plant, dreaming of Russia since the Cold War. Perhaps that's why I've never heard her speak a language other than English. Perhaps that's why I've never seen her passport.

Pathological lying is chronic. It's not the situation or the stress but an inner something. The pathological liar is not interested in scale, exactly, but staying within the limits of plausibility. To squeeze the tiny chick engulfed in your fist and feel the fluff on your palms, in your fingers, but not to crush it.

NAME:	Mother
BIRTH DATE:	June 6, 1945
BIRTHPLACE:	Unknown
FAMILY:	She was married before she married my father. My brother has a different surname. Which version of how she left her husband is better? She was pregnant with my sister and found flowers for another woman in his car. She only married him because her father disapproved of him, and they married too young. She found out he was bankrupt and walked out with my sister as a toddler. He was an alcoholic and she protected my infant sister.
OCCUPATION:	Perhaps she'd been lonely. A traveling salesperson drifting around England. Knocking on doors to convince people to please buy this vacuum cleaner, keeping these strangers talking long enough to collect details she could use to later invent other lives.

I still play the lying game when I visit my parents' home. My high score is thirteen in a week.

Did you drink the tea I made you? She says yes. (The cold mug, full, is still by the kettle.)

The name of the aristocratic lady she worked for changes three times.

One day her car was gone for a few hours and first it was grocery shopping but there was no food, and then it was visiting the farm over, and then it was the vet.

Did you go to the dentist? She says yes and she's going again next week. (She had promised my sister she'd get her rotten, broken teeth fixed for her health and for my sister's wedding. Her teeth are still black and my sister celebrates her seventh wedding anniversary this month.)

NAME:	Mother
BIRTH DATE:	June 6, 1945
BIRTHPLACE:	Unknown
FAMILY:	I haven't seen my brother since my sister's wedding almost a decade ago. He and my sister are close. I can count the number of times I've met him on my extremities. Sometimes when I'm visiting my parents I hear him call, and I hear my mother hang up. My brother tells my sister he doesn't know why. It's all a game of telephone. My brother was diagnosed with cancer several years ago and our mother lies when I ask if he's called recently: "Oh yes, I called him the other day, I might go up and visit them—the house is coming along nicely." My brother is at risk of forfeiting his mortgage because my mother has refused his pleas for financial help as his sickness has stolen his job.
OCCUPATION:	Perhaps it started in joy. A childhood love of magic and a glamorous career before children stopped her. Perhaps she pulled rabbits out of hats, mastered the Assistant's Revenge, maybe even the Aquarian Illusion. Perhaps she misses the magic so much she began daily illusions as a comfort.

My sister's own children are in the backseat and we haven't seen each other for six months. We talk maybe once a month. This is the closest we've ever been in almost thirty years. I don't know what to say when she complains that my mother lies about how much she helps with the grandkids. She asks, "Where does she even go all day that she doesn't ever want to see her grandkids?"

"The problem is," I tell her, "I just don't know her that well, which is a weird thing to say about your mother."

"Me either."

NAME:	Mother
BIRTH DATE:	June 6, 1945
BIRTHPLACE:	Unknown
FAMILY:	My sister and I only share genetic code on our mother's side. When people encounter us together the verdict is we don't share much at all. And it's true—we've never been the late-night phone call, share clothes, gossip-about-boys kind of sisters. She was four when my parents married and six when I was born. I've never asked about the life she shared with our mother before I arrived. I assumed she couldn't trust her child memory after the memories had been eroded by other stories.
OCCUPATION:	Perhaps our mother was someone else's mother entirely. Perhaps it was grief or longing or sorrow that pushed her to find solace in another life of lying.

I don't know exactly when my mother's first husband died. My sister and I had thought he was her biological father. The man my mother had left when she was pregnant with my sister or when she was a baby or when she was a toddler. When my mother refused to give my sister her birth certificate so she might know her biological father's medical history—a history my sister's own children carry within them—my sister repeated she just want to know the facts of the first husband, saying, "He's my biological father, right?"

My mother replied, "That's a story for another day."

THE SHOOT AND THE SHOW

I do not have a list of friends who have been punched in the face. In the temptation of binary—*there are two types of people in this world*—I have not considered this arrangement.

The list of people I have watched being punched in the face is extensive, and overwhelmingly male.

The list of people I have punched in the face is overwhelmingly male.

*

Mixed martial arts is the fastest growing sport in the world.

Despite this wildfire of popularity, MMA remains in the fringes of mainstream American culture. Senator John McCain, a lifelong boxing fan, called the sport "human cockfighting" and wrote all fifty governors, beseeching them to ban it. His wish was granted: MMA was banned virtually across the country until 2000, when, one by one, states began re-legalizing the sport. Still, New York holds out. Repeal on repeal has failed.

As a sport it is unfailingly, unflinchingly, macho.

The American masculinity that this machismo magnifies is largely measured in these terms: toughness, stoicism, acquisitiveness, and self-reliance.

*

One brief history of MMA: After Japan opened to the West in the mid-nineteenth century, the exchange was not only economic. A literal sparring, Japanese fighting styles taking on those of European and American fighters, gained credence.

Another. As the popularity of professional wrestling waned, it forked into two paths: the shoot and the show. Down the first path, a fight. Down the second path, a scripted performance of a fight, most notably the current incarnation of professional wrestling.

The shoot a real fight; the show a mere performance of it.

*

Not snakes, not lovers: something else writhing. Quantities unknown until the figures break and somehow there are only two bodies. The first five-minute round is over but they swirl back together almost immediately.

It is January in Massachusetts and I haven't seen this much skin in what feels like a decade.

I had no idea the first MMA fight I stumbled into was such a fine example. Jon Jones, Light Heavyweight Champion of the World, enters the cage for his eighth title defense against Daniel Cormier. I go back and forth from the couch to the kitchen, delivering hot tea to my sick boyfriend.

Jones goes for a choke—the needle of his arm threading through Cormier's shoulder, his neck. Cormier's head disappears. The crowd starts a chorus, but of course I don't understand what this closeness means. I don't understand the clinch, how when they lean together the weight becomes water to drown in. Yes, they are men hugging. Arms entwined until some imperceptible shift gets them unknotted into swift jabs.

At every interval I stay a little longer on the couch.

I only inch toward grasping the power of Jones's elbows. Mesmerized, already, by how his arms slip from fluid motion into angles I have only seen in punk music.

Cormier's corner yells only slightly louder than the crowd: "DC! DC! That's the dogfight I want. I want more activity. That's the dogfight I want!"

I stay put, the kettle cools on the stove.

The commentators declare this "a fight in a phone booth."

Into the final round, Jones stalks his prey. Cormier goes out flailing—a kind of wild I don't comprehend, wild like total abandon and thrill—a wild I have never read into the body.

✱

There are some things we refuse to understand as separate from our bodies.

Gender is often a crime of essentialism—a refusal to understand this identity as separate from the "facts" of biology.

As with most things we do not understand, they enrage us.

Kathy Acker writes, "In our culture, we simultaneously fetishize and disdain the athlete, a worker in the body."

This is a symptom, she states, of our continuing devotion to the dualism of Descartes. The self a perfect, crystalline thing against the body's changeable and volatile decay. Which is to say, the athlete violates a convenient division of self and flesh, body and mind.

A worker in the body. In this case, is the body the tool of labor or the labor itself? As we separate the self from body, we are told the self, too, is separate from its occupation.

We say all fighters are savages; we say all sex workers are victims. And yet, we do not disdain the construction worker, the trash collector, the farmer, for their bodies as labor.

Both *Psychology Today* and *Fight Club*'s Tyler Durden tell me, "You are not your job."

There is a veil that is drawn when the body works in certain ways. To enter the cage, a man becomes his archetype: the warrior. When a woman enters sex as labor, she becomes her archetype: the sex object.

These bodies play the roles we have assigned them for profit.

We are affronted by what our eyes have made.

*

Protect yourself at all times.

This is the primary rule of MMA. This is the commandment of the cage. Though the sport's marketing asks us to believe that there are no rules, this is not the case. But there are few.

At what point does a fighter learn protection as instinct? *Keep your hands up, keep your head moving!*

Protect yourself at all times: never walk alone at night, no headphones, don't leave your drink unattended, avoid drinking too much, remember to shout *Fire!* not rape. These are the protections that have been instinct for so long that I do not remember learning them.

*

MMA fighters must engage in fear management. Don't we all.

For a fighter, this emotional labor is likely to take one of three forms. Othering, in which the man in the cage imagines himself heroically superior or, conversely, his opponent as epically inferior, creates a gulf between the two fighters wide enough to allow belief in victory.

Scripting attempts to harness this gulf by the game plan, by the strategy, by the no surprises of nothing left to fate. This strategy hands the fighter a sense of control over the unknowable, something to repeat in calming rote, fingering a plastic rosary against the coming storm.

Both of these gulfs and the way in which a fighter may cross them, though, rely on the basic act of framing to build a defense against fear. Framing is essentially the act of definition, a technique that requires the fighter to look at the cage and ask, *What is this?*

This can give meaning to the most clichéd, hollowed out language. *This is just another day at the gym. This is my job. Win or lose, this is valuable experience. This is just another day at the office.*

But I wonder, when he looks to the cage and asks, "What is this?" should the fighter, instead, be looking in the mirror? Is the fear of loss or of injury (often conflated in the stakes of IV) an anxiety born of the body that will feel it, or the mind that will endure it?

*

Is there any space for boundaries within the fighter's body, when it is hewn so hard?

To cut weight suggests that the weight is already something extraneous to you. Superfluous meat. In MMA, this periphery to the body can be so significant that after weigh-ins a fighter will use an MMA drip to rehydrate.

The body must be controlled, whatever corner of the cage it is in.

My boyfriend tells me that the problem with American culture is that there is no tradition of asceticism (forgoing Thoreau).

An objection to this might be, *Well, the Puritans?* But Puritans were not ascetics, being focused only on certain restrictions in order to channel human energy to productive purposes—not the self-denial of all in order to reach the higher or spiritual realms of ascetics. The Puritan work ethic, not the ascetic transcendence.

I ask him, a former high school wrestler, what does that mean for the hunger you felt to make yourself smaller?

Were you a Puritan, denying the pleasures of food to enjoy the pleasure of optimizing your labor? The athlete, *a worker in the body.*

Or is the combat—cage or mat—some higher realm, a space of transcendence in which the man entering asks, "What am I?" and answers "Fighter."

*

Language obscures as it clarifies.

If the athlete confuses the boundary between mind and body, self and occupation, then we rely on language to re-create these borders.

When the worker in the body, the fighter, describes their action of the cage as labor or a spiritual existential experience, the effect is to exclude the alternate possibility. This might be self-evident: to be A is to not be B. A binary choice, whether it works in our favor or not, is calming in its finite range.

But what is self-evident might not provide us with truth: I think of the multiple MMA fighters adorned with a "God's Soldier" tattoo, this ink seemingly encapsulating both labor and spiritual possibilities. I think, too, of those lesser fighters already aging out and still throwing punches. MMA is a full-time job for a select elite; I am watching only the tip of the iceberg.

When I watch the fighter claim his prize, when I am comforted that he has been paid in full for his labor, I am satisfied not by hard work being justly rewarded but that the vast complex economy of the fighting body and the working body has been simplified into a formula that I can understand.

∗

Opening the documentary *Occupation: Fighter*, Josh Barnett, former UFC Heavyweight Champion, states, "Let's be honest, all forms of sports are just watered-down versions of war."

When Odysseus encounters a Phaeacian bard singing his own watered-down version of the Trojan War, he openly weeps. Lincoln reportedly wept upon hearing the "Battle Hymn of the Republic" for the first time, and then asked for an encore. Ulysses S. Grant sobbed for Lincoln's assassination.

At what point do a hero's tears make him less heroic? The tearless man takes the stage from those offering up their tears to battle during the Victorian period and builds that dominance into the twentieth century.

It is not unusual to see a fighter crumple to tears at the final buzzer. Relief or loss. High or low.

But to cry is a feminine failure. Or it is a failure of language.

When Kathy Acker describes her inability to describe the action of bodybuilding, she fails: "In a gym, verbal language or language whose purpose is meaning occurs, if at all, only at the edge of its becoming lost."

But this is not the case in the cage. While fear managed might make a fight "just another day at the gym," in performance language is not permitted to fail. The rituals must be observed: the trash talk, the prayer, *I just want to thank everyone for being here.*

When the final buzzer sounds, win or lose, a fighter is dragged back to language. Naked torsos are toweled off and covered in sponsorship slogans. The spectacle does not glitch: *What went wrong? Was that the game plan? So tell us, how does it feel?*

And the camera requires them to speak.

✳

Later in our domestic wars, a few years in, my boyfriend finally cries. He cries like an angry child, frustrated he cannot shackle the floodgates. It's hot and it's fast. It dumbs us. He cries until it is done. He cannot speak.

Conversely, my language loses all meaning. There is no point to be pressed, no argument to keep pushing. It falls to whispers; the licks of comfort, *It's okay, it's okay, I'm sorry,* curl around us, blank slips of paper.

The first time this happens I crumble at the sight of this cliff letting go inside of him. I had never seen him cry. My stoic, my sweetheart.

I think, *This is truly it, we are beyond language, we have arrived at love. This.* This is the shoot. His face blurred to the stark ballet of Sinéad O'Connor's tears in the "Nothing Compares 2 U" video.

Or he is Taylor Swift, the perfect breaking doll of "Blank Space." Clear eyes delicately mounted with tears. I'm the glassblower I watched every Saturday while my mother was in the market, gently shaping what is viscous to meaning with my lips.

These women perform sadness as a tragic beauty. A show of sorrow. In both of Roy Lichtenstein's *Crying Girl* pop art works, the blonde women are red-lipped and lacquered.

I have not experienced beauty in a man crying. I've been moved, say, by my father shedding tears at his sister's funeral, by Anderson Cooper breaking down while covering Hurricane Katrina; but these are somehow heroic.

And he returns to this place, and I follow with platitudes. Upon a repeat of tears, I get zero thrill. Instead of arriving at love, I am thwarted: my language is gutted of purpose and of poise. Irritated. I comfort as a machine. I think, *Is this how men feel when I cry?*

But relationships suffer destinations lightly. They pass, are encompassed, their streetlamps' light blending into the movie reel of memory. We do not arrive at any single moment without exiting it.

✳

A fight may be stopped for being too boring. Technically, failure to improve position. I dislike it when there is too much caution. For skill and beautiful movement, I like the technical fighters—quick leg trips, imperceptible realignment to put the opposition into submission. These tricks inspire the same gasps of wonder elicited the first time I saw a magician perform the Linking Rings illusion, breaking apart what I had believed to be solid.

In these moments—the stalemate, the clinch—I ache for rupture. My gaze wants its gratification. I think I'm joking when I yell, "Perform your gender for me!" at the screen.

I should take heed from the corner men yelling instead, "Do your job! Work!" at their charges. I should know the difference between masculinity and machismo. I should recognize the space between man and fighter, but in the spotlight of the octagon, I don't.

✳

An admission of guilt: when I say the body, when I've sung the body, when I've screamed it, it has never been gender neutral. The body of my work is always female.

What do I do to my own body, making it the spectator of this shoot, this show?

*

Those fighters that go beyond champions, those Hall of Famers, those big draws—those fighters who pry open your wallet for the pay-per-view—are not simply the best. They are the most entertaining. After his most recent fight (a victory marred by fan criticism of his methods), former welterweight champion Johny Hendricks laments, "I wanna put on a show for the fans, but I also have to win."

*

I am not the target demographic.

Commercials for the first UFC card included the slogan: "Two men enter. One man leaves." Women did not join the UFC until 2012.

I am not the target, anymore.

*

At the bar, I'm buzzed. I confess my dirty secret to a writer friend: I watch MMA.

He says, "I'm not interested in violence," as if violence is not a fundamental condition of being human. He hides his disdain, qualifies, "I loved professional wrestling as a kid, but for the melodrama, not the actual wrestling."

I explain how that is the show, and the thrill I get from the shoot.

"What is the point," he asks, "when there is real violence already, not sculpted for entertainment," and gestures to the TV, showing a muted stream of the Baltimore protests following the killing of Freddie Gray.

This is true—there is unconstructed violence available. If sports are a watered-down version of war, then a channel flip is all that's required to get war concentrate. We could move from the football field to the history classroom, and perhaps we should.

To be repulsed by a playing at war, sure. To be revolted by the thump of fist to face, of course. These reactions I understand. But uninterested? To not see the value of considering why it is he might be repulsed by one iteration and deeply saddened by another? That refusal is inhumane.

∗

On a recent trip to Brooklyn, I am elated to be reunited with one of my oldest and dearest friends. He knows it both: my shoots, my shows.

While discussing the violent outbursts of our hosts' once virile but graying cat, my friend lets slip some of my list: *That guy who cheated on your friend. That guy who cheated on you.*

The list of people I have punched in the face is overwhelmingly "that guy."

But I am not "that girl" anymore. I carefully cover up my first-generation college student, farm-raised, feral tomboy, fists-not-philosophy, uncultured face. I cover it up with the facade of someone who belongs in their company.

I dress it up with language.

∗

As language gives the fighter the tool to look at the cage and ask, "What is this?" it can also fail to adequately embrace the multitudes of an answer.

When Acker describes the gym as a hostile environment to "language whose purpose is meaning," she sells short the meaning garnered by the most repetitive, empty sentences.

This is my job. This is what I was born to do.

More importantly, even language stretched so thin of its meaning shouts loudly against any other potential meaning couched in silence. A quieter language of the body might contain more nuance than any our tongues might move toward.

*

The body can fail us in infinite ways.

In the cage, failure is quantified to knockout or submission. A particularly spectacular finish sees Jon Jones—pound for pound the best fighter in the world as I write this—submit his opponent in a standing guillotine choke. The two men are facing each other, and as the name implies, the aggressor tucks the head of his opponent into his armpit, driving his forearm into the opponent's throat. Apply pressure.

Though language might, in Acker's terms, fail, in the cage the body proves its own ways of speaking. To signify submission, a fighter taps twice to "tap out."

As we used to cry "Uncle!"

As we negotiate a safe word silly enough to be memorable: "Tractor!"

In this case, Jones's opponent refuses all language, and so slips from consciousness.

*

I have made the mistake.

(I have made him into anatomy; into meat.)

"Pound for pound" implies an impossible system of division that allows us to compare and contrast fighters across the spectrum of their weight.

In 2012 Jon Jones pulled out of the scheduled UFC 151 fight, stating that after fighting four times in ten months, he "felt like a piece of meat."

In response Dana White, UFC president, asked, "I wonder how the piece of meat was feeling when we bought him the Bentley."

The meat drives around at night. The meat abides the rules of the road, abides the rules so that the meat can continue to be meat. The meat sees the meat in the rearview mirror. The meat asks itself: Am I the body or its labor? Am I the self or the fighter?

.

ADORATION OF THE CLOSED MOUTH

I look to a mirror for a short history of false claims. Jan van Ruusbroec, a male mystic much influenced by Hadewijch in the fourteenth century, first damns the possibility of mystic experience (as opposed to mystic understanding of scripture) as that of doe-eyed children: "some people want to see God with their own eyes, as they see a cow, and they want to love God as they love a cow"; before opening up this still resounding refrain: "They sometimes have various kinds of images shown to them, both false and true ones. . . . Whoever makes much of this receives a great amount of it and in this way becomes easily contaminated."

This is to say women claim false experience of the divine. We of course know they make false claims of hell, too. The pervasive fear/conviction of the abundance of false rape allegations is staggering. Statistics vary but are generally held to be between 2 and 8 percent for *unfounded claims*. Unfounded is not directly analogous to false allegation. Alarmingly fluid, this can apply (but is not limited) to cases in which: *if the alleged victim did not try to fight off the suspect, if the alleged perpetrator did not use physical force or a weapon of some sort, if the alleged victim did not sustain any physical injuries, or if the alleged victim and the accused had a prior sexual relationship. Similarly, a report might be deemed unfounded if there is no physical evidence or too many inconsistencies between the accuser's statement and what evidence does exist.*

Or, experience called into memory via the female body is unstable. Uterine lining breaks down once a month, the unreliable narrator.

One friend raised Catholic and with a commitment to ritual if not a faith grew terrified as a teenager of the Immaculate Conception. Who would believe her if Jesus got her pregnant? Who would agree to a body untainted? I think this is wiser than I was at that age, to fear the consequences

71

you'll get, action or not. It's enough to fear what can happen even without touch. What is your body doing to the men. Are the men falling, the men are falling.

She says, "I think I am getting my period," as we wait for the man to arrive so we can order food. I used to be her roommate so I understand the apocalyptic intonation. I joke I am blinded by a vision of *The Shining* with its corridor crescendo of blood. The waves. It isn't funny. I hide this by offering some of the wackier theories regarding Kubrick's movie: it's a coded confession of his involvement in faking the moon landing. That bitch. That bitch, the moon.

In order to stabilize the body a girl might free it. Chisel the flesh to a perfect ice sculpture for your sister's wedding. In this way your cold thighs will not flesh, your flesh will not bloom, your bloom will not color.

One method for inducing saintliness in medieval women is to refuse menstruation (most easily done via starvation) and so the option is Madonna and not Whore. This trend has been named "holy anorexia." Not that the lithe, Christ-on-the-cross body is a desirable form, but rather that by eating only the body and blood of Christ, a woman can excrete miraculous substance. Of course, nothing *inside* her body could be defined as such. Only the things that are rejected, the negative space of her sacrificed figure.

Diminutive flesh might also be considered a dwindling investment. Catherine of Siena, holy anorexic, survivor of her dead twin, nurse to the most wretched, avoids her obligation as a family commodity (she was to marry her dead sister's widower) by ravishing her own beauty beyond repair. This takes a considerable amount of time. It is not enough to cut off her hair, scald herself, refuse any nourishment, reject sleep, beat with iron chains, stay silent. Time proves it. Or, seeing the marred daughter beyond marketable, the father releases his failed investment.

Catherine became a nun. Catherine became a bride of Christ. Catherine became part of the Sisters of Penance. Catherine became part of the Church. Catherine became distressed when her new family was divided by the Great Schism. Catherine became convinced her new family would listen to her reasoning of renunciation. Catherine became a totally closed mouth. Catherine starved herself to death. Catherine starved herself to death, a totally closed mouth. Catherine became a saint.

THREAD-WORK

When removed from another body, a thread is broken.[1] What we weave back together is a self. A kind of fate.

I was born wailing.

The first autobiography wept, already remote from the body.[2]

Ten days after the birth of Mary Shelley in 1797, Mary Wollstonecraft "expired at twenty minutes before eight."[3]

My father, sixty-two when I was born, wasn't there for my birth, but in all my childhood memories he is there, eclipsing my mother almost totally.

---

1. Nona, whose name means "ninth," was one of the three Fates in Roman mythology (the Parcae, equivalent to the Greek Moirai). Spinning the thread of life, she appeared to women in their final month of pregnancy.

2. Margery Kempe—the Christian mystic—dictated her unorthodox holy life, blessed with holy tears, in the fifteenth century. If you discount that the hands scribing were not her own, this is the first autobiography in English.

3. Wollstonecraft's husband, the philosopher William Godwin, in waves of grief, moved into her study, put her portrait on the wall, and wrote. His *Memoirs of the Author of "A Vindication of the Rights of Woman"* was published a mere six months after this expiration. Godwin's memorial sought to be a guiding light: "The justice which is done to the illustrious dead, converts into the fairest source of animation and encouragement to those who would follow them in the same career."

Wollstonecraft's thread broken, her husband weaves a tapestry to drape her memory in glory, to have her buried in a gown befitting an icon of freedom and reason. Instead, he dresses her with infamy.[4]

A friend of the couple, poet Robert Southey, accuses Godwin of "stripping his dead wife naked."

Mary Shelley comes to know her mother through her work, her writing, and the *Memoirs*. An unraveled corpus. Later, perhaps exhausted with the monopoly of Romantic male genius placed on autobiography, Shelley asks how a self is woven in *Frankenstein*.[5]

It's not that my mother died, but after our bodies unraveled from each other, we had little in common.

Wollstonecraft's legacy was marred not only by the scandalous content of the life Godwin wrote for her but also the complicated birth of a genre. Between autobiography, biography, and memoir, the Romantic period's growth of life writing threatened the borders between the male public sphere and the female domestic sphere. Wollstonecraft written out as a whore; Godwin, writing from the female sphere for a female audience, emasculated.

---

4. Godwin believed that it was not only Wollstonecraft's written works that presented a radical philosophical path but also her life. Her life as a work. A life that included several affairs without marriage, a possible triad with an already married painter, a daughter out of wedlock, two suicide attempts, and a resolute lack of remorse. The critical and public reaction to *Memoirs* was so inflamed, so scorching, that Wollstonecraft's work was buried with her body, setting back the cause of gender equality decades. Godwin was too grief-bound to attend the funeral.

5. "I feel exquisite pleasure in dwelling on the recollections of childhood, before misfortune had tainted my mind, and changed its bright visions of extensive usefulness into gloomy and narrow reflections upon self" (*Frankenstein; or, The Modern Prometheus* [New York: Penguin, 2013], chap. 2, pp. 47–48).

When I began to write my own corpus, I thought of it as weaving a new self. Somewhat secret, certainly far removed from family.[6]

In an age of all access, it's difficult to feel the depth of disgust felt by the reading public at being faced with the edited facts of Wollstonecraft's life and Godwin's willingness to write them. Though he quickly released a second edition to quell the tides of outrage, Wollstonecraft remained mired in obscurity. His memories, her forgotten.[7]

I had already left when my father started forgetting. The slippages coil— some snake back to the thread of memory easily, other strands are fully shed.[8]

As Godwin learned, to write a life is one thing; to edit that life, quite another. Somewhere is a list of the life I have not told my father.[9] It is too late to edit the one I have woven with him—he cannot grasp any new threads.

6. For most of my adult life, I have lived on one side of the Atlantic, and my family on the other.

7. In Mary Shelley's letters, Wollstonecraft is present not only as a specter but as an ominous yardstick. In September 1822, she writes to Mrs. Gisborne from Pisa: "How long do you think I shall live? as long as my mother?"

8. During my most recent visit with my family, my father would casually need to ask what day it was repeatedly. He forgot I where I was living. Yet other strands could be rebuilt. On forgetting, and being reminded of, my current living situation, he remembered the first time I'd moved to Atlanta, how he couldn't get over the size of the farm fields from the blurry phone photos I took whenever I traveled, how he always wondered what his life would've looked like if he really had been evacuated to Canada during the war, and how he didn't regret that he'd been kept in England.

9. This autobiography weeps.

NO APERTURE

In July the woman who does my nails shakes her head when I choose Black Knight. It is against season, unfeminine, and unnatural. With dark nails in the summertime, how will I ever become a fecund earth goddess?

Or, to dress a maiden in knight's clothing remains sacrilege.

Joan of Arc famously was executed on the charge of wearing men's clothing, her most heinous transgression in a list that ranged from horse theft to heresy.

Though cross-dressing in saints is not unusual, its acceptance varies wildly. Saint Theodora of Alexandria, a.k.a. Saint Theodore of Alexandria, in order to perform penance, disguises herself in male clothing so she might enter a monastery. What requires her penance is adultery; in order to pay for the sin of claiming sexual agency, she must dress as one who owns it.

Years later, still trapped by a lustful body but now Theodore, the monk spurns a local woman's advances. The scorned woman then accuses Theodore of fathering her child. Theodore, choosing to fall as a man, a more desirable result than being known as a woman, accepts the allegation. Theodore and baby are banished to the wilderness for seven years, but eventually are welcomed home. A man might work off his bodily sin, shuck it, unoriginal, so he can bathe purely in God's love.

The good woman is not the saint: one cannot be both unseen and seen. To become visible is an inversion of God-given order.

In a mystic theology of love, thirteenth-century mystic Hadewijch of Antwerp opined God as the knight opined his ladylove. A troubadour for Christ. When courted, the beautiful lady is silent and aloof, read as cruelty. The knight is spurned, the knight suffers.

The knight travels and faces obstacles in order to adore his love because he may leave his tower. He is the epitome of potential and promise. His lady may only perform in the role of love.

The implicit end game of joining—as absorbing two bodies to one—is for Hadewijch not without terror: "Of great Love in high thoughts / I long to think, day and night. / She with her terrible might / so opens my heart / I must surrender all to her."

As to fuck is a failure of boundaries, so the soul is annihilated at the height of experience with God. To become the Other, the self must vacate.

That Rapunzel can do nothing but submit to the man invading her tower under the cloak of love reminds us that both she and her hair are gold. Love as a form of commerce.

Perhaps if the lady could speak she would say *self-protection*, she would say *no*.

Both virginity and marriage are modes of hiddenness: unveiling oneself in either is scandal. Hadewijch marries Christ—but if she is the knight, and he is ladylove, Christ is the bride. Who lays down whom on a bed of heavenly flowers?

Despite being of monumental influence to Jan van Ruusbroec, himself a Flemish mystic well renowned both then and now, Hadewijch fell into obscurity. Perhaps, given her radical gendering as a bride of Christ, this is lucky, or perhaps it is only lucky that we do not know her fate.

For him, "Our satisfaction lies in submission to the Divine Embrace." Submission is a kind of order that those at the top might call natural.

He, with disciples and tagged *great, blessed*. The violence of footnotes.

When standing on the shoulder of giants, it is important to consider who has fallen from those great heights.

In the various formulations of the sublime as an aesthetic and philosophical category, there is often a return to great heights and abyss. The speck of man unable to comprehend his sudden lack of scale when faced with spectacular mountain views. Great poet unable to measure a pit into which he may not be romanticized for falling. The tower and its negation.

I'm not into the sexiness of the void.

Aristotle: "The female is a female by virtue of a certain lack of qualities."

When I was younger my mind built a strong and handsome wall of itself against the void. In medical terms this is called vaginismus, "a painful spasmodic contraction of the vagina in response to physical contact or pressure (especially in sexual intercourse)." My parents' doctor prescribed me Valium to take prior to sexual activity.

Jacques Lacan: "The lack is the lack of being properly speaking."

While in the wilderness, Saint Theodora is one of the Desert Mothers, a commune of asceticism. Refusal of everything that is not spirit. Refusal of food. Refusal of sleep. Refusal to shrink from pain. Refusal to fill the spaces vacated by flesh.

Amma, meaning "mother." Amma Theodora: "Do you see how humility is victorious over the demons?"

In the time I spend reading this wisdom of the *ammas*, I grow guilt. Knowing I should feel the stricture of their renunciation, instead I am more and more shocked by desert: How could I be so dry? How could my body endure itself, skin to skin, no lubrication?

The OPI nail polish collection Painted Desert includes shades entitled Sahara Sapphire and Nomad's Dream. This dream is a pinkish dirt color that I imagine is related to sand. The implication being a vastness so incomprehensible as to move straight through the eyes and into the subconscious.

Upon entering the eye, a grain of sand is regarded as a *foreign body*.

Lamont Classification of Vaginismus: "Level 1, the patient is noted to have tightness of the vagina but is able to relax with verbal encouragement. In Level 2, the tightness of the vaginal muscles is noted and the patient is unable to relax. A Level 3 patient avoids examination by lifting her buttocks off the table. In the most severe form of vaginismus, Level 4, the patient reacts by lifting the buttocks, retreating, and clamping the thighs together. Examination is usually impossible in Level 4 patients."

The austerities the Desert Mothers played on their bodies transfigure the hands holding their sexuality from the Church's to their own.

This early Christian period afforded significant independence to holy women, much to the chagrin of the Church. Considerable energy was put into enclosing them: the Council of Elvira legislated that widows must wear clothing by which they could be easily identified and take public vows affirming their widowed status.

Punishment of the female form is only punishment when administered in the natural order of man to woman. Grace Jantzen: "It would be an overstatement with more than a grain of truth to say that heretics were mystics who failed."

The invention of heresy is a historical event. While not singular, the hunt for heretics was fulfilled from the Middle Ages onward not by divine intervention or wrath, but because the hunters were defining and redefining the hunted.

As with any holy woman, the message is paradox: imitate / don't imitate.

Anointed but deviant from decreed existence—a miracle is a suspension of the natural order. Be awed, but do not be inspired to repeat.

Awe: rooted in the Old English word *ege*, meaning "terror, dread, awe," which may have arisen from the Greek word *áchos*, meaning "pain."

"The Alps fill the mind with an agreeable kind of horror," wrote Joseph Addison in his early work defining the sublime.

Though tensely related to the Romantics, Mary Shelley's *Frankenstein* is often held up as an exemplar of the sublime in the scale of its monstrous awe. Though Mother Nature has grown snakes for hair, she still moves high on her hips, curves in all the right places: Victor Frankenstein confesses "fervent longing to penetrate the secrets of nature."

A love of gothic is the same as any love of decoration. I often wear velvet as a protest against smoothed silhouettes.

When I was growing up, the most iconic nail polish was (and to some extent, remains) Chanel's Vamp. This deep red-black is evocative of Nefertiti, Queen of Egypt, staining her nails with henna and blood. Though a red lip links its cosmetic application to sex, supposedly conjuring the flushed gloss of the labia when aroused, the longevity of the appreciation of red nails appears less obvious. Originating in China, nail polish develops as a marker of social class: red becoming the pinnacle. As if having blood on your hands is a status symbol.

The warning colors worn by other women.

It is not until the 1930s that truly modern nail polish emerges with Revlon's revolutionary reapplication of car paint to smaller vehicles. Quickly, the spectrum expanded.

When he assigned *Frankenstein* in high school, my English teacher performed his own anatomization on the text, skipping chapters in favor of "the important bits." The way in which a woman may be divided into her most desirable parts.

Walton will ask of the Arctic: "What could not be expected in the country of eternal light?" The horror of constant vision. Three hundred sixty-six selfies a year.

We see ourselves in the surveillance state.

In 2013 my English teacher's son is one of the Arctic 30, arrested and detained in Russia on hooliganism charges after protesting oil drilling in the Arctic Circle. "A fervent longing to penetrate the secrets of nature."

I could not get my own fingers inside myself until I was twenty-two.

Being a shield or a flattened claw, a nail inside the body seemed unnatural. An alien threat. Something so hardened in what made me so soft. My vagina an echo of other parts pierced.

At what point does the body become artificial to itself?

A fingernail has been both self and Other for a significant period of human history. As with coloring them, artificial nails signal a difference of class, wealth.

In the early nineteenth century, Greek women of a certain class wore pistachio shells to lengthen their nails. I associate pistachios with a certain luxury. Prized hidden rewards, not already husked and needing to be repurposed. Opened and used up.

When is the onset of the pain? (before, entry, vaginal, deep, or after) I was born on a bridge, in the ambulance before it could reach the hospital. That part of the river is called "no man's land." One hundred sixty-six years before, Mary Shelley's miscarriage almost kills her: she is put in an ice bath to save her life. Thirty-two years before, Sylvia Plath will be married on this day.

Is it pruritic, burning, or aching in quality? When someone is sent to be burned at the stake and the fire is large, the cause of death is often carbon monoxide poisoning before flame damage occurs. If the fire is small, however, death might occur after the body has been burning for some time. Cause of death in this situation might be heatstroke, or shock, or blood loss, or simply decomposition.

Is it situational or positional? Burning is prevalent in many cultures, to the shame of the ashes marking foreheads at Easter.

Does patient have a history of STDs, especially HSV or HPV? [redacted]

Are there other sexual dysfunctions such as arousal, lubrication, or orgasmic difficulties? In that shame performs many functions for the body, one study suggests that men and women manifest it differently. Men shape their shame into anger and violence, whereas women, who are likely to feel more shame, sculpt it into introversion and self-loathing.

Is there any history of sexual or physical abuse? [redacted]

What we do to make belief easier. Mark our own hands, put the faces to different use *of our own free will.* Of course I wanted it. I am a goddess. Nothing holy has its will undone. I stopped breaking the line when I first wrote *rape.* I will not break any more of my bodies.

Vaginismus is defined as idiopathic—a condition whose cause is not known, or that arises spontaneously.

It could also be argued that involuntary muscle spasms when your vagina is approached for intercourse are not an insensible reflex. How our hands can move to shield without will. The eye's automatic shutting.

To be no aperture.

Blushing is also a natural reflex. Physiologically distinguished from flushing—a more concentrated red—it occurs in response to emotional stress. The blushing region has a distinct architecture in terms of blood vessels. A shame so internalized as to remain in the skin.

Because many women do not have adequate knowledge of their genital structures or function, giving the patient a mirror during the examination involves her in the evaluation process and provides education.

There does not exist a verifiable blueprint for the way in which memory shapes and reshapes itself after trauma. Though I do not remember the color of his eyes sufficiently beyond "brown," I can tell you that soon after the event I began to paint my nails in order to stop biting them while sleeping.

The lack, the lacquer.

Color is not unusual as a defensive strategy. For example, velvet ants (in fact, a type of wasp, though being wingless, the females resemble ants) are swathed in dense hair in a variety of colors—white, gold, blue, red—as a fair warning of their sting.

Hildegard, though not one of the tragic beauty martyrs (poor Rose of Lima scratching off her own mask for God), sees her holy things in color—sapphire or rutilant. *Rutilant* meaning "glowing or glittering with red or golden light." Christ's gut ruby on a crucifix. Though I think in her way, Hildegard is making a code for girls: *We bleed too. We bleed glitter.*

DIVISIONS OF THE BODY

Julian of Norwich has been in my dreams as a dead aunt on my father's side. For her, there are two natures in each person: their animal nature and their divine nature. She understands the normativity of being broken, how we are not looking to ascend or become at one within God, but to be less fragmented.

An impenetrable week passes. I see Julian every night, but she shows me nothing, and I can't think of a way to make these visions a punch line over coffee in the morning. I ask about your dreams.

I am mad at myself for appearing as if in a tower.

It has been almost five hundred years since Anne Boleyn's slender neck was split from the remainder of her body. It has been almost a year since I visited the site of this event. A small, manicured piece of lawn, respectful tourist label. She entered the Tower of London via the Traitors' Gate. In a wooing letter to her nine years before she got her block knocked off, Henry VIII begs, "If at any time before this I have in anyway offended you, that you would give me the same absolution that you ask, assuring you, that henceforward my heart shall be dedicated to you alone. I wish my person was so too."

Multiplicity in a woman is unreliable weakness, for a man it signifies scope and responsibility. He cannot be solely promised to her person because he is too important. Of Henry's schisms this one is not original.

Anne, I am sorry I did not feel an echo at the site of your death.

Among the many significant convictions Western thought inherited from the Greeks is this: the body will tell you no higher truths. Beginning with Pythagoras's convenient Table of Opposites we learn that *female* is akin to oblong and plurality as well as to curved and to darkness. It is no major philosophical breakthrough for the body to become only female, and the mind, male.

The most threatening obstacle in a woman's path to sainthood is multiplicity of allegiance. One woman cannot be both daughter and wife, cannot marry Christ when already sold, must choose Beyoncé or Rihanna, waxed or natural, Taylor or Miley, sweet or sultry, prude or slut, full fat or diet, work or family, cherry or vanilla, grunge or preppy, clever girl or party girl.

In a family of sisters, the primary anxiety is creating further categories beyond "the smart one," "the pretty one." After number five (the odd one) the parents have no more children for fear number six would lead to multiplicity.

The truth about sisters is that they are people. The truth about people is that they are men.

You learn how to make your face move right. When finally watching *Carrie* for the first time among others at age twenty-four, I did the grimace then the gratitude for not being her. In the kitchen getting more popcorn, I wanted to ask every girl I'd met if her mother told her the blood was coming.

Aristotle calls me "a mutilated male."

He calls me cold, but I run hot most of the time, hotter on my period. My dreams get semifevered.

Marguerite Porete, a mystic, was burned at the stake in Paris for her heretical writings of the Freed Soul—and the stations that we, the marred, must go through to enter this estate.

Later, for Marguerite, the soul will say, "I have lost my name in order to love." Like O in the *Story of O*, forgoing or transcending subjectivity, nothing more than mask and an arrangement of orifices. A book too scandalous to have been written by a woman, a love letter.

If one is never marred how does one become whole? The hermetically sealed body, the perfect man. If one has always been whole with no becoming do you know your wholeness? I think of this when trying to be more accepting of my mutilation. I have often thought this while throwing blood-marred panties in the trash.

A CASE AGAINST PATHOLOGY

Opening Remarks

It's the age of true crime, and women are the focus and the fuel. We have an obsession with podcasts whispering about serial killers on our commutes, detailing homicidal domestic disputes as we buy our groceries, reciting rapists' rap sheets as we review our to-do lists, until finally we get home and put on the latest documentary with graphic images of violence in order to relax.

It's easy to get caught up in the language of epidemic—addiction, infection, bingeing—when it comes to the millennial woman's obsession. A language that points toward the underlying cultural discomfort with true crime as "chick lit." What's wrong with these women? What sickness compels an appetite for Bundy and Manson and Dahmer? Like the appetite for novels that drove Victorian women to be abandoned to asylums, true crime's popularity among women pushes toward pathologizing.

When a cultural trend leans toward women, "I like it" ceases to be a full sentence. Instead, a *because* is required, a thesis statement to open a justification. Nowhere is this clearer than when women consume violence.

True crime's recent resurgence in podcasts such as *My Favorite Murder*, *Sword and Scale*, and *Up and Vanished* is often traced to the explosive popularity of the "original" true crime podcast, *Serial*, which debuted in 2014. The audience for these podcasts is overwhelmingly female. While academic studies confirm this assertion, I already knew this from the whisper network of women in my life—admissions or recommendations often prefaced with the hesitance of "I know it's weird but . . ." or "I don't know if you're into *this sort of thing* . . ."

Such popularity is trailed by a continuing rash of headlines asking, with increasing shrillness: *Why do women like this?* Implicit in this question is a disbelief in the compatibility of women and violence, and further, that women need a justification for their cultural consumption.

This current question is nothing new. True crime's initial flourishing as a genre in the 1970s and 1980s prompted the same question, to the extent that true crime's rise was connected not only with the development of the interstate highway, which created ideal conditions for serial killers, but also with the women's liberation movement, which created the surprisingly ideal audience for such narratives.

Back further, and further still, this need to couch violence as suitable for women's consumption only with a *purpose* echoes.

EXHIBIT A

Before I came to true crime, there was hagiography. Same itch, different scratch.

Although I lost any remnants of childhood faith long ago, the lives of the saints, particularly female saints, fascinated me. These stories were often repetitive—beautiful young woman, noble, willing to sacrifice herself through starvation or torture or celibacy for her love of God. The stories of virgin martyrs in particular stoked my gruesome interest. Saint Agnes, Saint Margaret, Saint Juliana . . . they begin to blur together in their pious but bloody ends. These legends, and the religious iconography that accompanies them in medieval churches and on Catholic saint dictionary websites, were deliberately homogenous. The martyrs' resemblance to each other, as well as to Christ, so erased their individual difference that by the fifteenth century virgin martyrs were represented in art with their torture in order to distinguish between this litany of dead girls: Saint Apollonia carries her pulled teeth, Saint Lucy displays her plucked eyes on a platter.

Though these women blurred together, the ending was always the same: a corpse.

∿ Saint Euthalia

Initial observations: Upon entering the family home in third-century Leontini, Sicily, on August 27, witnesses observed the body of a young woman in the house atrium, approximately three feet to the left of the main entrance. The body was partially clothed in an underrobe of blue fabric and a robe of red silk with gold trim, torn to reveal the victim's shoulders and left breast. A large reddish-brown stain surrounded the body, proceeding from the neck. Victim's head was not connected to the body and was found approximately three feet away, in the northeast corner of the atrium. A sword was observed, likely a *spatha* with a straight blade roughly thirty-five inches long. This weapon was placed on top of the victim's torso. The scene appeared to be that of a homicide.

Upon medical examination, victim was identified as Euthalia, sister of Sirmilian, daughter of Eutropia, the Christian convert who attributed her recovery from dysentery to Jesus. Cause of death, decapitation. Profile of the neck wounds matches the profile of sword found at the scene.

Victim determined to be a virgin.

Initial interviews with family confirmed a violent domestic dispute occurred. According to Eutropia, she had previously left the family home after Sirmilian threatened her with strangulation.

Sirmilian confirmed his mother's description of events. Sirmilian further confessed to killing his sister, striking her neck with the sword identified at the scene. According to Sirmilian, his sister angered him after she reproached him for threatening their mother.

In his statement, Sirmilian described the initial altercation with the mother and his sister's defense of Eutropia's Christian faith. In response Sirmilian asked, "Art thou also a Christian?" Euthalia answered, "Indeed I am, and am ready to die for my Lord."

Sirmilian then stripped his sister and beat her with his fists. This statement is consistent with bruising found on the victim. He confessed he intended to give Euthalia to his slave to be raped, but Sirmilian claims that his sister prayed and the slave was "struck blind" before any sexual contact occurred. Sirmilian confessed to beheading Euthalia, stating "that bitch shamed my house with that talk, and mocked me with her disobedience—it was the last straw."

~ Edmund Kemper, a.k.a. the Co-Ed Killer

Excerpts taken from an "Interview with Edmund Kemper," March 1974.

Just a few hours after California's mass murderer Edmund Kemper, twenty-four, was convicted on eight counts of first-degree murder, he kept a promise and granted me an exclusive interview.

[...]

As a sex-starved young man in what should have been a peak of his virility, he was sexually and socially so uncertain of himself that he began to prey on hitchhiking coeds, not as a rapist, but as a murderer and necrophiliac.

"At first I picked up girls just to talk to them, just to try to get acquainted with people my own age and try to strike up a friendship," he had told investigators. Then he began to have sex fantasies about the girls he picked up hitchhiking, but feared being caught and convicted as a rapist. So, he said: "I decided to mix the two and have a situation of rape and murder and no witnesses and no prosecution." [...]

On the witness stand, though, Kemper testified that "death never entered as a factor" in the coed killings. He said: "Alive, they were distant, not sharing with me. I was trying to establish a relationship and there was no relationship there.... When they were being killed, there wasn't anything going on in my mind except that they were going to be mine ... That was the only way they could be mine." (Kemper testified that as a child of eight he had killed his pet cat, which had transferred its affections to his two sisters, "to make it mine.") [...]

Kemper did not kill again until after he bought a .22-caliber pistol in January [1974].

"I went bananas after I got that .22," he told me.

The day he bought it he fatally shot coed Cynthia Schall, a nineteen-year-old Santa Cruz girl, in the trunk of his car. He carried her body into his mother's apartment near Santa Cruz, kept it in his bedroom closet overnight, and dissected it in the bathtub the next day while his mother was at work.

He buried the girl's head in the backyard "with her face turned toward my bedroom window and, sometimes at night, I talked to her, saying love things, the way you do to a girlfriend or wife."

Less than a month later, Kemper picked up two girls, Rosalind Thorpe, twenty-three, and Alice Liu, twenty-one, on the campus of the University of California at Santa Cruz (UCSC). He shot them both to death in the car before driving off campus and later cut off their heads in the trunk of his car while it was parked in the street in front of his mother's apartment.

Kemper's final killings were those of his mother, Mrs. Clarnell Strandberg, fifty-two, and her best friend, Mrs. Sara Hallett, fifty-nine, in his mother's apartment on Easter weekend. Then he began a cross-country flight, in a rented car loaded with guns and ammunition, that ended in a decision to surrender, "so I wouldn't kill again."

EXHIBIT B

I struggle to distinguish the medieval predilection for portraying martyrs with long, oval faces from Bundy's penchant for long hair with a center part. The parade of perfect martyrs marches right on through history, taking on each era's peculiar beauty standards to arrive as today's parade of perfect victims.

Before Kemper murdered his mother and turned himself in, he preyed on hitchhiking college students, picking them up in his yellow 1969 Ford Galaxy outfitted so that the passenger door would not open from the inside. These young women could once have been saints.

The dead girls of true crime have inherited more than death from their hagiographic foremothers. There is specifically, a *look*. Like the martyrs made so similar that they had to be painted with the instruments of their torture, the victims of the most voraciously consumed true crime narratives are those that fit a paragon of victimhood: bright-eyed, slim, white, middle-class, at least one description as a good girl. A picture of innocence.

And the picture matters—true crime narratives, like the lives of saints, are inherently visual. In an interview with true crime scholar Laura Browder, one publisher explained: "Pictures are at least 60 percent of the initial draw and you can't sell a paperback if you don't have solid pictures. This may seem trivial, but it is a key issue because what makes a book different is that it delivers the things you can't get anywhere else. This includes things like the autopsy pictures, the severed breasts of prostitutes, the slashed throats—things you'll never see on TV." Even now, with true crime's dominance of the podcast medium, the genre relies on graphic visual descriptions of violence. But its trueness, that single syllable precursor, is what protects true crime from the charge of aestheticizing violence. As in, *I didn't compose this scene, but let me conjure the exact angles of the Black Dahlia, let me explain how her body was severed at the waist, intestines tucked under the buttocks—an almost postmodern scene of fragmentation.*

Despite the protection of "truth," true crime cannot fully escape the charge of stylizing violence. There is an editorial hand at play—choosing which dead girls to spotlight, which mutilations to maneuver into the script. The same editorial hand, no doubt, that nudged monks to shift the details of a martyr's imprisonment from her bedroom to a dungeon, her torture to flesh hooks rather than fists.

And yet, for all the niche motives and means of violent crime, for all the increasingly lurid photographs, all these narratives end up, like their victims, looking the same.

EXHIBIT C

The uniformity of these narratives, the bloody but predictable formula followed by both the saintly and the criminal, might offer the key to their popularity.

The repetitive nature makes consumption easy, unnoticeable. I've consumed whole seasons of storytelling in an almost fugue state—entranced until emerging hours and hours later with only vague memories of the case's details remaining. I've exhausted the same cases with different voices, buzzing the Manson family murders in my ears via the podcasts *Young Charlie; You Must Remember This; Last Podcast on the Left; Cults; Hollywood and Crime*—and still clicking subscribe to any new treatment of the same doomsday cult details.

This bingeing is not unique to the audio format. Laura Browder, in her study "Dystopian Romance: True Crime and the Female Reader," observes that true crime books tend to be hefty tomes and that "readers tend to read them 'like eating popcorn,' as one reader put it—consuming a great number of pages, or even the entire book, at a single sitting."

But the ability to mainline multiple murders or martyrs in one session does not explain the specific appeal of these narratives to women.

More than the repetitive soothing of comfort food, true crime, no matter how heinous the villain or bizarre the crime, follows a familiar path.

This formula has been reinvented from its eighteenth-century origins of the criminal biography, tweaked to include developments in science, and even fine-tuned to fit highbrow literary expectations. But the fundamental variables endure. The true crime narrative is no secret: one or more crimes, a few red herrings, a break in the case, and the arrest and imprisonment, sometimes death, of the criminal.

Perhaps women are drawn to these formulaic narratives because of their drive toward justice; after all, Blind Justice is a woman. Or perhaps the clear narrative arc, predictable even in perversity, cuts through the messiness of navigating the world as a woman. No gray areas: just right, and very, very wrong. A distinct path, even if it is a bad one.

EXHIBIT D

Genre trouble as gender trouble might be a story as old as murder.

Although medieval women could not write, they could commission hagiographic texts—an agency to shape and share the stories they consumed—and so the lives of female saints form a specific genre within that dubious literary genus of *women's literature*. Meaning, a genre written and consumed by women: the original chick lit.

Whatever the specific condescension of the label, the designation is clear—the *women* under the status of *literature*. Most often narratives that explore relationships, love, and domesticity with a female protagonist are slotted into this box. As if human drama, when considered through the lens of the fairer sex, is made frivolous. As if *Don Quixote* is not about love or *Robinson Crusoe* about loneliness.

The rise of the novel, and particularly its escalating female readership, caused an all-out moral panic in eighteenth-century England. Who would care for the children if the women were reading? What depravity would ensue in the dirty house left by the novel readers? If women read of the interior lives of others, would they desire their own? This novel reading was viewed as a threat to the patriarchal structure not only because time spent reading was time that should have been spent performing the gendered work of the *angel of the home*, but because of the desire to *consume*. That the novel was authored by men positioned these women as vampires—insatiable succubae sucking the life from male authorship.

When women read, the whole genre they consume is diseased and must be diagnosed.

True crime, with its overwhelmingly female audience, has so far resisted designation as *women's literature*. Perhaps because the authorship of true crime does not display the gendered skew of its readership, or perhaps because the perspective of true crime's protagonists comes from a body bag.

Yet hagiography and true crime are yoked together under that ultimate breed of women's literature: romance. The story is so familiar as to be cliché. Boy meets girl. They fall in love. Obstacles ensue. Then, an aisle, or a beach, or a courthouse. A ring and a promise, and it's all over for a happy ending.

Or is it? Scholars of both the lives of saints and true crime point to their genres as a continuation of romance, following what happens *after* the wedding. For saints, their marriage to Christ is sabotaged by a vengeful father or lover—or Christ is the lover for whom they refuse the proposals of earthly men, and in anger, the earthly men kill to prevent the celestial union. In true crime, Browder argues, the drive toward desire follows a similar downfall: "While the formula for the romance novel entails the pursuit of a woman by a domineering, masculine lover, and ends in marriage, the true crime book typically picks up where the romance novel leaves off, and exposes the controlling, sexually dominant male as a dangerous killer."

That there will be a dead girl is a narrative inevitability. This is the truth that true crime offers, the truth offered by virgin martyr narratives. A truth that fills the plot holes in the story that's been sold to women for centuries: the story of the happy ending, the story of the successful life, the story of girl to bride that ends at the fairy-tale wedding and leaves the rest to the horrored whisper of rumor.

EXHIBIT E

In searching to answer the overplayed question of *what women want*, current pundits of true crime's popularity overwhelmingly return to the answer: *information*.

"Captured by True Crime," a much-cited 2010 study by Amanda M. Vicary and R. Chris Fraley, describes the popularity of true crime among women rather than men, "the more aggressive sex," as a "paradox." I have to wonder, if true crime's audience demographic was skewed in a more male direction, would there be no questions worth pondering? In examining this paradox, Vicary and Fraley conclude through multiple test methods that women read true crime as a means of survival. That is, women read true crime in order to learn what not to do.

This wisdom runs the gamut from the rallying cry of *Stay sexy and don't get murdered*, to the more familiar *Never put both headphones in*, to the unexpected *If you're trapped in the trunk of a car, urinate to leave* DNA.

In another study, a true crime fan states she chooses reading material in order to learn how to avoid raising serial killers.

Such didacticism runs straight to the heart of what exactly true crime *is*. Ian Case Punnett, in his *Toward a Theory of True Crime Narratives*, traces the fundamental split between true crime and its genre cousin, journalism, as due to the presence of the author. Both are committed to presenting facts, but journalism has developed an honor code of objective truth—the journalist just a tool of the story. True crime, in contrast, has no qualms about carrying a moral or a message.

Or true crime fascinates female readers as another iteration of conduct literature. A genre as old as time, your basic instruction manual: the book of *how should a woman be*.

Dead women have always been the narrators of such guidebooks. While in the lives of female saints their deaths are the beginning of their eternal lives rather than their earthly end, the aim of these hagiographies was, as Catherine Sanok argues in "Reading Hagiographically," to "present idealized feminine behavior and encourage female audiences to adopt it." It is extraordinary that in an age with a literacy rate of almost zero and extreme patriarchal restriction of women's access to ideas that a whole genre, directed at a female readership, flourished. Less shocking is that in order to make the message of modesty, piety, and chastity palatable to the explicitly female audience, the writers of these guides to womanhood included the most gruesome depictions of mutilation, torture, rape, and, of course, murder.

∿ Saint Catherine of Alexandria

Initial observations: upon clearing the crowded Alexandria town square, the body of an extremely emaciated young woman was identified on November 25, 305. The body was approximately two-thirds covered by multiple wounds, most concentrated on the back and chest, the result of scourging—likely inflicted by a *flagrum* or *flagellum*, a short whip made of two or three leather thongs. Given the abrasions evident, these lacerations were inflicted over a prolonged period—likely during imprisonment. Further weapons collected from the town square include what appear to be the fragments of a spiked breaking wheel. As expected, the woman's head was separated from her body due to sharp-force trauma, the result of this public execution.

The corpse was quickly identified as Catherine, daughter of the governor, Constus. Catherine is well known in Alexandria as a Christian, as well as a noblewoman. Recent incident reports in this precinct cite Catherine as an instigator of religious unrest—the previous twelve religious executions in Alexandria, including of the former empress, occurred a short time after Catherine orated on the Christian faith. Her recent notoriety, as well as her social status as an eligible virgin, made this execution very well attended. Catherine was previously apprehended and imprisoned for her heretical faith, and Emperor Maxentius reportedly handed down this death warrant after advanced interrogation techniques (specifically the scourge and the wheel) failed to yield a renouncement of faith or an affirmative answer to his proposal of marriage.

Members of law enforcement were called to the scene not as a result of Catherine's death but to provide crowd control for the civil unrest. Onlookers described a chaotic scene: "It seemed like it was going to all get cleared up when the emperor offered his mercy and to marry her—but she said she was already married to Jesus, and that's when all hell broke loose."

Witness interviews suggest that this disruption began after Catherine herself called for the execution to begin, and after the executioner complied, an unidentified, milklike substance "flowed from her neck." Samples have been taken. However, a clean sample was difficult to obtain as officers were unable to collect the blade at the scene. The crowd of onlookers rushing the executioner's platform resulted in a severely disrupted crime scene.

~ David Parker Ray, a.k.a. the Toy Box Killer

> Excerpts taken from the transcript of audio tapes David Parker Ray played
> for his victims after kidnapping and imprisoning them in Elephant Butte,
> New Mexico. The content of these graphic tapes is widely available on the
> internet. Ray was apprehended after Cynthia Vigil escaped by overpowering
> his complicit live-in girlfriend, Cynthia Lea Hendy. Publicity surrounding
> the case prompted other women to come forward, including Angelica
> Montano. Montano had reported her kidnapping and torture to local police,
> but no investigative follow up occurred. Further survivors from the area,
> who wished to remain anonymous, also came forward with accusations
> of multiple accomplices, including law enforcement. He was convicted on
> charges of kidnapping and sexual torture but died by heart attack before his
> trial for murder. It is believed that Ray may have killed up to sixty women.

Hello there, b*tch. Are you comfortable right now? I doubt it. Wrists and an-
kles chained. Gagged. Probably blindfolded. You are disoriented and scared,
too, I would imagine. Perfectly normal, under the circumstances. For a little
while, at least, you need to get your sh*t together and listen to this tape. It is
very relevant to your situation . . . I don't know the details of your capture,
because this tape is being created July 23, 1993, as a general advisory tape for
future female captives. [. . .]

Now I'm sure that you're a great little piece of a*s and you're gonna be
a lot of fun to play with, but I will get tired of you eventually. If I killed every b*tch that we kidnapped, there'd be bodies strung all over the country.
And besides, I don't like killing a girl, unless it is absolutely necessary. So
I've devised a safe, alternate method of disposal. I had plenty of b*tches to
practice on over the years, so I've pretty well got it down pat. And I enjoy
doing it. I get off on mind games. After we get completely through with you,
you're gonna be drugged up real heavy, with a combination of sodium pen-
tothal and phenobarbital. They are both hypnotic drugs that will make you
extremely susceptible to hypnosis, autohypnosis, and hypnotic suggestion.
You're gonna be kept drugged a couple of days, while I play with your mind.
By the time I get through brainwashing you, you're not gonna remember a
f*cking thing about this little adventure. You won't remember this place, us,
or what has happened to you. [. . .]

If it has not already been done, very shortly a steel collar is going to be
padlocked around your neck. It has a long, heavy chain that is padlocked
to a ring in the floor. The collar will never be removed, until you are turned

loose. It's a permanent fixture. The hidden playroom, where you're gonna be kept, has steel walls, floor, and ceiling. It is virtually soundproof and has a steel door with two keyed locks. The hinges are welded on and there are two heavy deadbolts on the outside. The room is totally escape proof, even with tools. Anytime that you are left unattended in the room, your wrists will be chained and there are electronic sensors to, uh, let us know if you move around too much. And if that's not enough, there is a closed-circuit TV system with a surveillance camera. It's wired to the main TV in the living room so we can check you once in a while, or just sit and watch you for the fun of it. Electronics is a wonderful thing. Expensive, but hell, everything in the room is expensive, and damn well worth it. If everybody knew how much fun it was to keep a sex slave, half the women would be chained up in somebody's basement. [...]

Okay, let's talk about, uh, your training, the rules and punishment. Here, you are a slave and discipline is extremely strict. You're gonna be given a set of rules, things you can and cannot do, and you will learn to comply because each time you violate a rule, you will be punished. As soon as each rule is told to you, it will become law as far as you're concerned. And you know what's gonna happen every time you f*ck up. We'll use a couple of methods of punishment. A whip is an excellent training aid, so is an electroshock machine. Anytime you get out of line, one or both will be used on your body, and I assure you, it will not be pleasant. There is not many rules and they're very easy to remember. But you're gonna make mistakes. Every slave does. I don't like repeat offenders. It gets me very upset. [...]

I cannot predict the future. I can't predict changes of procedure. But if this tape is being played for you, I have to assume that it is still reasonably accurate. And I can only give you advice. Be smart and be a survivor. Don't ever scream. Don't talk without permission. Be very quiet. Be docile and obedient, and by all means, show proper respect. Have a nice day.

EXHIBIT F

Any survival guide contains two paths: the written *Do this and you'll make it*, and the unwritten *If you don't do this, you'll fail.*

Saint Catherine is among the most popular of the virgin martyrs—and though she is held up as paragon of virtue, withstanding her incarceration, starvation, and sexual harassment with grace, we know she has to die. She refused her father's instruction, she refused the institution of marriage, she spoke when she should have listened. She failed as only a woman can fail.

The threat inside every survival guide functions to keep us on the path. Saint Catherine keeps us on the path of good Christian women; Little Red Riding Hood keeps us on the main road home; Gary Ridgway, the Green River Killer, keeps us from stopping on the Pacific Coast Highway.

True crime presents women these paths in negative, but the binary remains. Like the exemplars of saints or the fables of fairy tales, true crime narratives are a type of regulatory fiction.

These are the stories we are told, and begin to tell ourselves, about the acceptable ways to perform gender. And within these stories is a darker tale, the tale of what happens if you stray from the path, a tale that shows us the victim is at fault for whatever happens because she didn't follow.

Although true crime is clear in its messaging—whether that be *Don't accept rides from strangers* or *Play dead after the first slash of a knife*—as a genre its political agenda can be cloudy. For all that examinations of violent crime often puts the spotlight on toxic masculinity and is skeptical of the supposed safety of traditional family structures, true crime can also uphold traditional patriarchal structures of authority.

Is true crime empowering women to be prepared against any threat, or threatening them to be prepared?

EXHIBIT G

What if true crime teaches us nothing at all?

If the dead girls marching from martyr narratives into today's mania for murder are not here to educate us, what are they here for—and why do we keep inviting them? Why do I keep inviting them in? Reading the fatal traumas of other women might not school us on how to avoid trauma but retreading the trauma of others might provide a means to confront our own.

At the heart of trauma is a void. The outline is clear—we can trace its shape, feel for the smooth and rough parts. We would recognize that shape even in the dark. But what that border encases: nothing. The hole of nothing, the depth of nothing, the gaping vast goneness.

Traumatic memory is shaped in this abyss. In trauma theory, it is called "the missed moment": a memory we return to, inescapably, to confront, only to fail and return again, and again. Like the survivors of David Parker Ray, whose memories of his "toy box" torture were obliterated with a careful chemical cocktail, we will come back to our missed moment—in dreams, at unexpected junctures, unbidden—even if we are uncertain that this trauma took place.

The rote details of another body's trauma echo, depth-sounding like a stone dropped down a dark well to determine just how deep. The repetitive formulas of true crime, of the lives of saints, become an avalanche of pebbles to fill in the void.

The concept of relief through horror is as old as the basic tenets of narrative—both received from Aristotle. Though no lover of women, Aristotle, it seems, understood the allure of gore. Catharsis: the purging of strong emotion via art. That is, the trauma of others purges our own, for a while at least. And if we do not want an opportunity to relive our own traumas and survive, at least art gives us an opportunity to feel out the limits of horror—to have a belief in boundary restored. If we read about one more serial killer, we might finally know the worst of what can happen. If we read one more murder, one more rape, one more arson, one more molestation, one more spree of armed robberies. Just one more, just one more, and then the depth of humanity's evil will no longer be able to surprise us.

CASE STUDY: Mutilation

∿ Saint Agatha of Sicily

Initial observations: Upon entering the cell in which the deceased was held in the Catania, Sicily, detention center, on February 5, 251, officers noted significant signs of decay. The body was found housing significant insect activity, obscuring a more exact time of death. However, the presence of maggots but not flies suggests death occurred between two to ten days previously. Due to the deceased's incarceration, identification was made quickly by correctional officers: Agatha.

This OK was further corroborated by the significant wounds sustained by the deceased. While decomposition prevents a comprehensively accurate catalog of wounds, the corpse shows significant abrasions likely inflicted by scourging, disjointed shoulders and knees likely the result of torture on the rack, and burn marks covering approximately 40 percent of the corpse. Most significantly, Agatha was identified by the unusual chest wounds, the result of a forced double mastectomy. These wounds appear severely infected.

The deceased had been imprisoned under the auspices of Roman prefect Quintianus. Before presiding as the judge in the heresy case of Agatha—a professed Christian—Quintianus pursued Agatha romantically, proposing to the avowed virgin on multiple occasions, both before and during her imprisonment. Witnesses at the trial recall Agatha refusing Quintianus's proposals, turning her back on the judge and crying, "Jesus Christ, Lord of all, you see my heart, you know my desires. Possess all that I am. I am your sheep: make me worthy to overcome the devil."

Autopsy was unable to ascertain exact cause of death but did confirm that Agatha was pregnant at time of death. This pregnancy is likely the result of rape. Prior to the deceased's final imprisonment, she was sentenced to incarceration in Aphrodisia's brothel for a month. No witnesses were forthcoming with further information about this time.

⌒ Jerry Brudos, a.k.a. the Lust Killer and the Shoe Fetish Slayer

Excerpts transcribed from episode 79 of the podcast *My Favorite Murder,* "Sharpest Needle in the Tack."

My Favorite Murder bills itself as a comedy true crime podcast, but such a label fails to encompass the "murderino" phenomenon it unleashed. Begun in 2016 by Karen Kilgariff and Georgia Hardstark, the podcast, with a simple format of friends sharing their lives and then swapping a true crime story each, quickly gained millions of listeners by putting women front and center. Frank discussions of mental health, a focus on victims, and the refusal to apologize for their grim fascinations has created an almost teenage sense of comradery.

At the crest of true crime's new wave of popularity, the show's tag line of *Stay Sexy and Don't Get Murdered* now adorns merch, echoes at sold-out tour venues, and is exchanged between strangers in recognition of displayed fandom.

In the episode "Sharpest Needle in the Tack," Kilgariff tells Hardstark the case of Jerry Brudos, a serial killer and necrophiliac who killed at least four women in Oregon between 1968 and 1969. Introducing the case, Kilgariff describes Brudos's traumatic childhood, and her story is punctuated by Hardstark's exclamations, commentary, and occasional cursing.

After Kilgariff speculates about how possible alcoholism on the part of Brudos's parents was the cause of his almost-itinerant childhood and describes the abuse the young Brudos endures, Hardstark quips: "How to create a serial killer!"

Jerry Brudos's first murder victim was named Linda Slawson. Employed as a door-to-door encyclopedia salesperson, she arrived at the Brudos home on a rainy January evening in 1968 with hopes of a sale:

GEORGIA HARDSTARK: No, no, no, no, no, no, no—that sounds like a horror movie.
KAREN KILGARIFF: Completely. The way this is written it's like she's trying to decide: she hasn't had any sales, she's just moved out on her own.
GH: She's gonna keep trying, maybe the next one.
KK: She needs the money, she has to eat, things are getting bad. There's one last house that has a light on and she's like, "I just want to go home. I'll just try this one last time."

Both hosts then take a detour from the narrative to imagine themselves in Slawson's shoes. Although it remains unspoken, you can hear Kilgariff and Hardstark's own experience of balancing the "risk" of moving through the world as a woman with the need to survive.

Returning to the case, Kilgariff hones in on the moment Slawson rings the doorbell and is met by Brudos:

KK: When you see a picture of him, he looks like a cartoon. He looks like the missing friend on *King of the Hill*. He looks like a grown-up Charlie Brown with army-issue black glasses on. Just a big, round head.
GH Like pasty.

KK: No distinguishing features.

GH: A little lumpy.

KK: Yeah. Almost like a bit of a snowman—just round, round, round.

They pile on to Brudos—making fun of his appearance and lumpishness with pointed laughter, as one would a friend's terrible ex-boyfriend or creepy boss. Kilgariff then tells Hardstark how Brudos, met with the "opportunity" of Slawson's presence while his wife is out of the house, convinces Slawson to enter his workshop. Brudos hits her over the head with a two-by-four before strangling her to death. As a "product killer," Brudos is not motivated by the process of killing, however, but by the corpse itself:

KK: After she's dead and before he gets rid of the body, he takes off her clothes and dresses her up in the stolen underwear that he has in his collection. Then . . . this is bad. He cuts off her left foot and keeps it in the freezer in a high-heeled shoe.

GH: No! I'm just processing that . . . holy shit! That is crazy.

As Kilgariff explains how Brudos later fakes a flat tire on the Wilsonville bridge in order to dispose of Slawson's body in the Willamette River, Hardstark continues to have difficulty processing the bizarre and horrific image of the foot in the freezer.

As is often the case with serial killers, Brudos's behavior quickly escalates:

KK: Then, in July 1968, six months later, Stephanie Vikko is reported missing from Portland. Then in November the same year, Jan Susan Whitney is reported missing from Portland. Jan is a twenty-three-year-old college student at the University of Oregon. Then in March 1969, so about six months later, a woman named Karen Sprinkler, who was a nineteen-year-old college student, goes missing. When the police take the eyewitness accounts of Karen going missing, two young girls tell the police they saw a large man dressed as a woman on the parking lot garage roof where Karen's abandoned car was found that day.

GH: Whoa.

Once again, the hosts step out of the narrative in order to put themselves into the situation, with Kilgariff imagining the ploy of dressing as a woman as a means of luring women into safety—a ploy that Hardstark admits she would fall for.

Kilgariff's pacing of the narrative reflects the accelerating momentum of the serial killer's increasingly frantic behavior, as she recounts the continuing escalation of April 1969. Brudos attempts to abduct Sharon Wood, a student at Portland State University. Wood fends him off by biting his thumb and drawing blood. Though Brudos beats her unconscious, a car comes and Brudos flees. The next day, Brudos attempts to abduct fourteen-year-old Liane Brumley in his car, but she escapes. Brudos's final known victim is reported missing less than forty-eight hours after this adduction, on April 24:

KK: . . . a woman named Linda Dawn Salee is reported missing. Her car is found abandoned in a parking garage. The police realize now that they're dealing with a serial killer. So the next month, which is May 1969, a local fisherman discovers Linda Salee's body in the Long Tom River. It was weighed down by a car transmission. And then two days after that, Karen Sprinkler's body is found fifty feet away.

GH: Oh my God.

KK: So that's obviously his dumping ground. Karen was also tied to an old engine, which is the reason it kept her submerged for a long time. And he, this is bad . . .

GH: Okay.

KK: He cut off her breasts to keep as souvenirs. He also placed a bra from his collection of undergarments over her mangled chest. This guy is basically berserking: he's killing, he's trying to attack women almost daily, killing people, and then these bodies are coming up. It's just all going faster and faster.

Kilgariff moves on to describe Brudos's "berserker mode" and the desperate methods to find victims that would eventually get Brudos caught, accompanied by expressions of incredulity on Hardstark's part:

KK: So the same month he starts calling dorm rooms at Oregon State University to try to arrange blind dates with the coeds.

GH: What the fuck?!

KK: And it works.

GH: No.

KK: Uh-huh.

GH: What does he say?

Unable to comprehend this absurdity, the hosts dissolve into laughter.

EXHIBIT H

The question of *What do women want?*, with regard to true crime, comes down to boundaries. Is there a limit to horror? Is there a limit to knowledge?

Like the universe, the limits of horror are ever expanding—its edges creeping further and further into depravity. No amount of garish paperbacks, brutal documentaries, or indecent podcasts can keep up with crime, and no amount of crime stories can truly transform us into the perfect survivor.

Once we have walked through that door of *nothing left to learn*, through the door of *reliving and replaying our own traumas*, we arrive back where we started—a world in which, as Browder writes, "women fear violence, but are culturally proscribed from showing an interest in violence." A world in which a woman should gracefully tip her face into her delicate hands when the blood begins to pool on the screen, should look away from the news with a slight shake of her head rather than stare down the sirens and the slaughter.

The same slaughter and the same sirens that soundtrack every military history, every new hot take on the world wars, every nonfiction book with a blurb of "gritty," every Oscar-bait drama praised for its "graphic realism." Where is the diagnosis for these media sensations?

The answer, of course, is our standard double standard. Men's interest in violence is permissible because men's desires are self-approving. Want it? *You got it.* Want to read a pop history of a generic genocide? *Great choice, sir.*

Closing Argument

The aim of diagnosis is twofold: search and destroy. Although the term's Greek stem *diagignoskein* means only "to know thoroughly," we have layered on another clause to complete that sentence: to know thoroughly in order to correct. It is not enough to know the cancer—it must be cut out.

True crime's rapid rise in popularity is not a cultural epidemic but rather another symptom of a longstanding plague. Disease mutates, takes on different manifestations, perhaps even different hosts, but at root it remains the same malady.

A malady that mutates misogyny into concern trolling: *It's not that murder is unladylike, I'm just worried for your well-being.* This choice to actively consume, rather than passively absorb, the violence inflicted on us as women threatens the natural order of paternalism, the still swaying undercurrent that men's violence is theirs alone to deal with: to inflict, to portray, to protect us from.

The threat blooms that we might press pause, consider the horror, and continue.

ACKNOWLEDGMENTS

Many thanks to the editors of the following publications, in which these essays first appeared:

Bayou: "The Arsonists"
Beecher's Magazine: "The Double King"
Black Warrior Review: "No Aperture"
Conjunctions: "I Am a Burning Girl"
Diagram: "Reliquary"
Fairy Tale Review: "The Discomfort Index"
The Map Is Not Territory: "Union"
Mid-American Review: "Divisions of the Body"
Missouri Review: "What I Should Consider before Weeping in Frustration at Airline Customer Service after a Six-Hour Delay on My Honeymoon"
Pleiades: "Adoration of the Closed Mouth"
Prairie Schooner: "Vacation"
Quarterly West: "Boys on the Radio"
Seneca Review: "Thread-Work"
Sycamore Review: "The Shoot and the Show"
Texas Review: "Origin Unknown"

It is a particularly strange corridor to walk down, trying to write *thank you* during a global pandemic. Remembering all the folks who have made this book, who have made me think, is eery as nostalgia always is, but taken to the extreme, as they all feel so painfully far away.

First, thank you to Alexander Chee, for seeing this manuscript as a book, and to all the folks at the University of Georgia Press for making this possible. Thank you to the editors who published these pieces originally, and thank you especially to

Tommy Mira y Lopez of *The Map Is Not Territory* for your work in commissioning and shaping "Union." Thank you too to Eula Biss for choosing "The Double King" for the Agnes Scott Literary Festival Prize—your kind words and advice over cold cuts helped shape this book immeasurably. Thanks to everyone we met on the road trip described in "The Discomfort Index." All of your dive bars were exactly the same and exactly perfectly unique. Thank you for the beds, the couches, the breakfasts, and the beers.

I'm indebted to so many talented and kind readers. Thank you, Corinna Cook, for reading some of these essays in upstate New York. Thank you to all the folks at Georgia State who worked through some of these pieces in that magical nonfiction workshop. To everyone in GSU's Department of English, endless gratitude. In particular, Josh Russell and Dr. Beth Gylys, I am so grateful to have been gifted such kind, supportive teachers. It is wild to call so many friends colleagues, and I am especially thankful to GSU for weaving the following people into my life: Ashe Prevett, Megan Clark, Nora Bonner, Cora Rowe, Mary Ann Barfield. To all of my students at GSU, you have been the reason to keep going more often than I can count. For your grit, humor, and questions, thank you. Atlanta truly influences everything.

Thank you to Linzy Barnett, the best therapist a gal could wish for and likely the real reason I could write this book. And to the folks at Unit 2 Fitness, especially Ryne, who have made me strong in more ways than one.

Endless gratitude to my partner, Cyrus. In this book you became my husband, and you husbanded this book. Thank you for being the soundboard for early thought experiments, your chicken-scratch notes on first drafts, and your absolute support in writing the life I share with you. Thank you for making space in that life for me to write and for holding me through the long silences when I wasn't ready. For always being inappropriately proud of me, thank you. You are stubbornly good. I love you.

I am so grateful to my in-laws, Lisa Joyce, Jim Parlin, and Ursula Parlin. Thank you for your unwavering support. It is difficult to fully express the extent of my dumb luck in finding not only a partner but a family. Your kindness and curiosity are topped only by your humour. Thank you especially, Jim, for including "Boys on the Radio" in your process for *Sweater Set Eurydice*.

To my parents, thank you. To Lucy, I wish you knew how much you impress me, how much I look up to you, even from far away.

Friends, you are not friends. You are my family.

To those who were there for the events of this book, for the writing of it, for the recovery from it, for the before and after and the right now, thank you for being with me. Christeene Alcosiba, Meredith Blankinship, Caitlin Creson, Hannah Doyle, Anna Sandy-Elrod, Annie May Taylor, Gale Marie Thompson: you ladies are saints.

Nick Sturm and Carrie Lorig: I love you, for burning the lyric, for burning Christmas trees, for being people who burn with so much more love and vision than this world deserves.

To Kit Emslie, my heart-twin, thank you for everything. Literally, *everything*. From Scotland to the American South, you are my partner, my absolute safety, my gut check. For the puns, the macarons, the proofreading, thank you. Most of all, for the blue shadows, the azure seawater.

To the witches of western Massachusetts: Molly McArdle, Caroline Belle Stewart, and Zoe Rana Mungin, you are the fuel and the fire. We lost our friend Zoe in April 2020. She died from Covid-19, after being refused treatment. She was a talented writer, beloved teacher, and fierce advocate. Zoe, I have tried to measure it, the heft of your absence, and it is immeasurable.

This book is for her.

NOTES

In addition to the individual hagiographies I consulted, I am deeply indebted to the following collections: Sarah Gallick, *The Big Book of Women Saints* (New York: HarperOne, 2007); Catherine Mooney, ed., *Gendered Voices: Medieval Saints and Their Interpreters* (Philadelphia: University of Pennsylvania Press, 1999); Cristina Mazzoni, *Saint Hysteria: Neurosis, Mysticism, and Gender in European Culture* (Ithaca: Cornell University Press, 1996); and Grace Jantzen, *Power, Gender, and Christian Mysticism* (Cambridge: Cambridge University Press, 1995).

Reliquary

This essay is partially an ekphrastic response to the *Twelve Apostles Altar* (Zwölf-Boten-Altar), painted by Friedrich Herlin of Nördlingen, 1466, which depicts the circumcision of Christ. I am indebted to David Farley's 2006 *Slate* article "Fore Shame." A slight apology to Leo Allatius—his work as a scholar and keeper of the Vatican Library far outshines his unpublished minor essay "De Praeputio Domini Nostri Jesu Christi Diatriba" ("Discourse on the Foreskin of Our Lord Jesus Christ").

I Am a Burning Girl

The phrase "the holocaust of ballet girls" was first used as the title of an 1868 article in the British medical journal *The Lancet*. An excellent history of the young women who died as a result of their tutus catching alight from gas lamps is the chapter "Inflammatory Fabrics: Flaming Tutus and Combustible Crinolines" in *Fashion Victims: The Dangers of Dress Past and Present* by Allison Matthews David (London: Bloomsbury, 2015).

The *Museum of Broken Relationships* is an original creative art project conceived by Olinka Vištica and Dražen Grubišić in 2006 and has since expanded to exhibitions around the world, with permanent locations in Los Angeles and Zagreb.

Context for the femicide at Salem is drawn from Carol F. Karlsen's *The Devil in the Shape of a Woman: Witchcraft in Colonial New England* (New York: Norton, 1998).

The Discomfort Index

The reference to my introduction to Greek and Roman myths that portrayed the sexual violence therein as an offering of comfort is Philip Freeman's *Oh My Gods: A Modern Retelling of Greek and Roman Myths* (New York: Simon & Schuster, 2012).

The Double King

The common modern version of "One for Sorrow" goes: "One for sorrow, Two for joy, Three for a girl, Four for a boy, Five for silver, Six for gold, Seven for a secret never to be told."

An earlier version of the nursery rhyme, which is still very much in use, goes: "One for sorrow, Two for mirth, Three for a funeral, Four for birth, Five for heaven, Six for hell, Seven for the devil, his own self."

What I Should Consider before Weeping in Frustration at Airline Customer Service after a Six-Hour Delay on My Honeymoon

This essay is heavily indebted to Heather Christle's *The Crying Book* (New York: Catapult, 2019) and the years of crying wisdom that built this work. The history of Britishness and tears is superbly explored by Thomas Dixon in *Weeping Britannia: Portrait of a Nation in Tears* (Oxford: Oxford University Press, 2017).

Many tears were spent in frustration as an undergraduate and in later years much comfort gained by spending time with *The Book of Margery Kempe: A New Translation, Contexts, Criticism*, edited and translated by Lynn Staley (New York: Norton, 2001).

The study whose media reception was lamented by coauthor Noam Sobel is Shani Gelstein et al., "Human Tears Contain a Chemosignal," *Science* 331, no. 6014 (2011). Jacob M. Vigil's 2008 study is "Sex Differences in Affect Behaviors, Desired Social Responses, and Accuracy at Understanding the Social Desires of Other People," *Evolutionary Psychology* 6, no. 3.

Information on the crying clubs of Japan was drawn from Patrick St. Michel's article "Crying It Out in Japan" in the May 2015 issue of the *Atlantic*.

It is impossible to overstate how indebted I am to Seamus Heaney as a poet and thinker on history and one's complicities within it. The quote about his relationship to Catholicism is from Frank Kinahan's 1982 "An Interview with Seamus Heaney" in *Critical Inquiry*.

Ian Rankin's Inspector Rebus is quoted here from *Black and Blue* (London: Orion Books, 1997).

The thread of Roy Lichtenstein in this essay is indebted to Deborah Solomon's 1987 *New York Times* article "The Art behind the Dots."

Vacation

This essay was written in 2015, the year I graduated from my MFA program at UMass Amherst, and explores the racial trauma endured by the writer and social studies teacher Zoe Rana Mungin. Zoe died in 2020. Her death was the result of Covid-19 and the deeply racist medical system that does not take the pain of black women seriously. Zoe was turned away twice for testing, and she passed away after over a month on a ventilator. She was thirty years old.

The review of the Go-Go's is from the September 9, 1982, edition of the *Columbia Daily Spectator*.

Joan Mitchell quotes are taken from Patricia Albers's excellent biography *Joan Mitchell: Lady Painter* (New York: Knopf, 2011).

Sexual violence statistics are from Patricia Tjaden and Nancy Thoennes, *Extent, Nature, and Consequences of Intimate Partner Violence: Findings from the National Violence against Women Survey* (Washington, D.C.: U.S. Department of Justice, 2000). Notably, this research has not been updated by the U.S. Department of Justice in the intervening two decades.

The Arsonists

Eudora Welty is quoted from "The Art of Fiction No. 47" in the *Paris Review* 55 (1972).

Thanks to Molly Brodak for telling me the Brothers Grimm tale "Straw, Coal, and Bean."

Union

This essay draws much of the background information on Cyrus West Field from Bill Burns's "History of the Atlantic Cable and Undersea Communications: Cyrus W. Field," Atlantic Cable, updated December 30, 2019, atlantic-cable.com/Field. The telegraphic exchange between Queen Victoria and President Buchanan is housed in the digital archive of the Library of Congress Prints and Photographs Division.

Background information on the history of spousal immigration was drawn from Sabrina Balgamwalla's 2014 article "Bride and Prejudice: How U.S. Immigration Law Discriminates against Spousal Visa Holders" in *Berkeley Journal of Gender, Law, and Justice* and Janet Calvo's "A Decade of Spouse-Based Immigration Laws: Coverture's Diminishment, but Not Its Demise" (CUNY Academic Works, 2004).

Many thanks and apologies to Leslie Diaz, the Atlanta immigration lawyer who shepherded my green card application, and who read this essay with generous frustration.

The Shoot and the Show

I am deeply indebted to Dr. Jay Rajiva's reading of this essay, and to conversations trying to theory the body.

"The American masculinity that this machismo magnifies is largely measured in these terms: toughness, stoicism, acquisitiveness, and self-reliance" is driven by Rebecca Clay's "Redefining Masculinity" in *Monitor on Psychology* (2012).

Further ideas of masculinity, from baseball to cowboys to skyscrapers, are hugely indebted to the work of Michael S. Kimmel, particularly *The History of Men: Essays in the History of American and British Masculinities* (New York: State University of New York Press, 2005).

All Kathy Acker quotes and ideas embedded here are from "Against Ordinary Language: The Language of the Body" in *The Last Sex: Feminism and Outlaw Bodies* (New York: Palgrave Macmillan, 1993).

The section that explores fear management draws much from this article: C. A. Vaccaro, D. P. Schrock, and J. M. McCabe, "Managing Emotional Manhood: Fighting and Fostering Fear in Mixed Martial Arts," *Social Psychology Quarterly* (2011).

Adoration of the Closed Mouth

Jan van Ruusbroec quotations are from *The Spiritual Espousals*, translated by James A. Wiseman (Mahwah: Paulist Press, 1985.)

Language and statistics surrounding false rape allegations are indebted to this study: David Lisak et al., "False Allegations of Sexual Assault: An Analysis of Ten Years of Reported Cases," *Violence against Women* (2010).

For considerations of anorexia mirabilis, Caroline Walker Bynum's *Holy Feast and Holy Fast* (Berkeley: University of California Press, 1988) and Rudolph Bell's *Holy Anorexia* (Chicago: University of Chicago Press, 1987) were invaluable. As were the insights of Mary-Ann Barfield.

Thread-Work

In thinking about the genre of autobiography and memoir, Felicity Nussbaum's *The Autobiographical Subject: Gender and Ideology in Eighteenth-Century England* (Baltimore: Johns Hopkins University Press, 1995) has been instrumental.

I am grateful to Dr. Lindsay Eckert for her expertise on the Romantic shaping of memoir, for the discussions on Godwin and Wollstonecraft, and the generous feedback on working through these ideas in other forms.

No Aperture

The title of this essay is a response to Susanna Kaysen's *The Camera My Mother Gave Me* (New York: Vintage, 2002).

Excerpts from Hadewijch's "Of Great Love in High Thoughts" are taken from *Hadewijch: The Complete Works*, translated by Mother Columbia Hart (Mahwah: Paulist Press, 1980).

Quotations from Jan van Ruusbroec are taken from *The Spiritual Espousals*, translated by James A. Wiseman (Mahwah: Paulist Press, 1985).

Aristotle is quoted in Simone de Beauvoir's introduction to *The Second Sex* (New York: Vintage, 2015); for the passage in question, see Aristotle's *Generation of Animals*. Jacques Lacan is quoted from *The Seminar of Jacques Lacan, Book II: The Ego in Freud's Theory and in the Technique of Psychoanalysis, 1954–1955*, edited by Jacques-Alain Miller, translated by Silvana Tomaselli (New York: Norton, 1991).

Amma Theodora quotes are from John Chryssavgis, *In the Heart of the Desert: The Spirituality of the Desert Fathers and Mothers* (Bloomington, Ind.: World Wisdom, 2008).

On nail polish, fingers, and manicures of all kinds: Angus Trumble's *The Finger: A Handbook* (Melbourne: University of Melbourne Press, 2010).

"It would be an overstatement with more than a grain of truth to say that heretics were mystics who failed" is from Grace Jantzen's *Power, Gender, and Christian Mysticism* (Cambridge: Cambridge University Press, 1995).

Quotations from Mary Shelley's *Frankenstein; or, The Modern Prometheus* are taken from the Penguin Horror edition, 2013.

Medical information about vaginismus is drawn from the following sources: Tessa Crowley, David Goldmeier, and Janice Hiller, "Diagnosing and Managing Vaginismus," *British Medical Journal* (2009); Cherng-Jye Jeng et al., "Management and Outcome of Primary Vaginismus," *Journal of Sex and Marital Therapy* (2006); Yitzchak Binik, "The DSM Diagnostic Criteria for Vaginismus," *Archives of Sex Behavior* 39 (2010); and David Bode, Dean Seehusen, and Drew Baird, "Dyspareunia in Women," *American Family Physician* (2014).

Divisions of the Body

Henry VIII's love letters to mistress and wife Anne Boleyn were collected and published by J. W. Luce in the 1906 volume *The Love Letters of Henry VIII to Anne Boleyn*, digitized by Harvard University in 2007.

Aristotle is quoted from *On the Generation of Animals*, trans. Arthur Platt (Oxford: Blarendon Press, 1910).

Marguerite Porete is quoted from *The Mirror of Simple Souls* (Notre Dame, Ind.: University of Notre Dame Press, 1999).

A Case against Pathology

Excerpts taken from "An Interview with Edmund Kemper," by Marj von Beroldingen, *Front Page Detective Magazine*, March 1974.

Excerpts from the transcripts of audiotapes made by David Parker Ray (a.k.a. the Toy Box Killer) from "Thinking about Philosophy" (thinkingaboutphilosophy .blogspot.com), audio published at *True Crime Magazine*.

The transcript excerpts from Georgia Hardstark and Karen Kilgariff's *My Favorite Murder*, episode 79, "Sharpest Needle in the Tack," were edited for clarity. In clarifying further details of the Jerry Brudos case, I relied on the timeline published by Radford University's Department of Psychology, available at http://maamodt.asp.radford.edu/Psyc%20405/serial%20killers/Brudos,%20 Jerome.htm.

Laura Browder's work was invaluable to my thinking about true crime: "Dystopian Romance: True Crime and the Female Reader," *Journal of Popular Culture* 39 (2006). As were Ian Case Punnett's *Toward a Theory of True Crime Narratives: A Textual Analysis* (New York: Routledge, 2018); the study by Amanda Vicary and Chris Fraley, "Captured by True Crime: Why Are Women Drawn to Tales of Rape, Murder, and Serial Killers?," *Social Psychological and Personality Science* (2010); the article by Kelli S. Boling and Kevin Hull, "*Undisclosed* Information—*Serial* Is *My Favorite Murder*: Examining Motivations in the True Crime Podcast Audience," *Journal of Radio and Audio Media* (2018); and Rachel Franks's article "True Crime: The Regular Reinvention of a Genre," *Journal of Asia-Pacific Pop Culture* (2016).

On hagiography and conduct literature: Catherine Sanok, "Reading Hagiographically: The Legend of Good Women and Its Feminine Audience," *Exemplaria* (2001), and Katherine J. Lewis, "Model Girls? Virgin-Martyrs and the Training of Young Women in Late Medieval England," in *Young Medieval Women* (New York: St. Martin's, 1999).